WONDER AND ...

WONDER AND WISDOM

*Conversations in science, spirituality
and theology*

CELIA DEANE-DRUMMOND

DARTON · LONGMAN + TODD

Dedicated to my daughter
Mair Clare
born on 6 December 2005
the feast of St Nicholas

First published in 2006 by
Darton, Longman and Todd Ltd
1 Spencer Court
140–142 Wandsworth High Street
London SW18 4JJ

ISBN 0 232 52591 9

A catalogue record for this book is available from the British Library.

Designed and produced by Sandie Boccacci
Set in 10.25/13pt Sabon
Printed and bound in Great Britain by
Page Bros, Norwich, Norfolk

CONTENTS

ACKNOWLEDGEMENTS

I WOULD LIKE TO express my sincere appreciation to the John Templeton Foundation, without whose support this book could never have been completed. I am particularly grateful to Paul Wason, whose encouragement and feedback during the application process proved invaluable. The John Templeton Foundation awarded me a grant for a sabbatical leave in the second semester of 2004/2005, during which time I completed this book.

I would also like to thank my colleagues in the Theology and Religious Studies Department at the University of Chester, whose support for a sabbatical leave in the first semester of 2004/2005 enabled initial research for this book to be carried out. During this study period I had occasion to draw on the resources of a number of libraries, including the John Rylands University Library, Manchester, St Deiniol's Library in Hawarden and Oxford University libraries. I am particularly grateful for the support offered by staff at St Deiniol's Library. This library, as in the past, has offered me a particularly stimulating yet supportive environment while working on this book. I am also grateful to Rev. Dr Margaret Yee for the invitation to research the works of Austin Farrer that are held at Oxford University.

While this book was in preparation, I had the privilege of giving a number of lectures and sermons that drew on the material that is covered in this book. These are, in particular: a sermon at Nuffield College, Oxford, on 4 February 2005; an address given as part of the Lent series on science and religion at St Mary the Virgin, Warwick on 27 February 2005; a lecture given at a study day on Holy Wisdom for the St Theosevia Centre for Christian Spirituality in Oxford on 23 April 2005; a lecture entitled 'Finding Wonder, Seeking Wisdom' given for the 93rd Annual Conference on Religion and Science for the Modern Churchpeoples's Union on 14 July 2005; and a seminar entitled 'How does experiencing wonder in living creatures relate to a theology of wonder and beauty?' for the Science Symposium for the C. S. Lewis Summer Institute on 'Making all Things New: the Good, the True and the Beautiful' on 4 August 2005. The comments and questions I received from these various audiences helped me in the preparation and completion of this book.

I would also like to thank Virginia Hearn of Darton, Longman and Todd, whose enthusiasm for this project from its inception was very encouraging to me. I would also like to thank Liz Piercy, who helped with the production of this book while Virginia was on maternity leave.

INTRODUCTION

W$_{HAT}$ $_{HAS}$ W$_{ONDER}$, that apparently innocent feeling of amazement so common in little children, to do with wisdom, often thought to be the privilege of those who are old? What has theology and religious experience to do with scientific investigation of the natural world? This introduction sets out to introduce the themes of wonder and wisdom, and to show how exploring these themes raises new and interesting questions for the dialogue between science and religion. It also points to a form of spirituality that is integrative of the world around us, rather than detached from it. Both wonder and wisdom are common to religions other than Christianity. However, rather than explore such religious traditions here, I will show ways in which our biologically evolved nature lends itself to the development of such traditions. Different cultural traditions will shape the particular content of what wonder and wisdom might mean, but understanding these in the light of the evolution of life shows ways in which humanity is predisposed to develop such traits. In addition, our ability to pay attention will influence our capability for both wonder and wisdom.

WHAT IS WONDER?

In what sense is wonder appealing? Wonder can mean different things for different people. The experience of wonder might arise because of a contradictory and amazing situation or event, one that seems to destabilise the existing order of things. On the other hand, wonder could also be the experience of those who reach a sense of perfection in the ordering of the world.[1] What might be called beauty might accompany both experiences, although wonder as destabilising could also be associated with the so-called 'monstrosities' in the natural world. In any case, historically so-called wonders marked the outermost limits of what might be 'natural', while wonder as a passion showed the limits of human knowing, presenting to the human mind something previously unknown. This is one reason why the emotion of wonder is so often associated with childhood; a child constantly has new experiences, and so has a renewed capacity to wonder at such boundaries. Wonders could also be what medievalists called preternatural, that is situated at the boundary of the miraculous and the natural.

The emotion of wonder has its own history. Its roots are in the Indo-European word for 'smile'. Natural philosophers of the ancient world interpreted wonder as the response to something not just rare or unfamiliar, but also when something happened through an unknown cause. Aristotle believed that wonder was the source of inspiration for a philosopher, for following such an experience the search could then begin for causes. He believed that wonder was important at the beginning of philosophy, but it had little to do with what he understood by curiosity.

In the twelfth and thirteenth centuries, the literature blurred accounts of sacred and miraculous events with the secular and marvellous. Wonder could mean a mixture of fear, reverence, pleasure and bewilderment. Medieval writers believed that the outer limits of the known world were a place where wonders accumulated, full of exuberant natural transgressions. In this way, for medieval writers wonder was more about a realisation of ignorance. This was in stark contrast to curiosity, which, in the natural realm, they believed was a somewhat ambiguous and negative desire to know the secrets of nature. Such secrets should not concern those who seek after God. Augustine reinforced this by mounting a vitriolic attack on curiosity; at best it was futile, at worst a distraction from God and salvation.[2] He associated curiosity with the vices of lust and pride. Yet he was rather more positive about the value of wonder. He argued that even what we might find commonplace is still full of wonder, as God is the Creator of all that is. He also tried to prove Hell existed by pointing to the existence of wonders. Augustine helped to create an important shift in what wonder means. Instead of simply being associated with the frivolous and pleasure rooted in the experience of novelty, wonder came to be linked with the feeling of religious awe.

The Christian literature of the period embraced all kinds of natural wonders as a source for divine inspiration. Those who reflected on the creation in this way had a duty to attribute its marvels to God, the Creator. Vincent of Beauvais, writing in 1240, for example, described the created world as like a mirror, so that virtually everything in the created world became capable of eliciting wonder. While Augustine still held a view of wonder tinged with fear, Vincent's view was more pleasurable. By the thirteenth century, writers distinguished between the exotic as the outcome of natural causes, and the monstrous, associated with divine intervention. If someone encountered the exotic, then this would lead to appreciative wonder. If, on the other hand, someone encountered the monstrous, this would lead to more fear-laden feelings of wonder associated with divine portents. Wonder came to have the connotation of astonishment and admiration by the late fifteenth and sixteenth centuries. Yet, only the elite experienced the tradition of wonder at this stage in history.

By the sixteenth and seventeenth centuries wonder came to be associated with curiosity. Hobbes believed that curiosity was the attribute that distinguished human from beast, but whereas lust could be satisfied, this was impossible with curiosity, and hence it should be linked with greed, not lust. Unsated curiosity gave rise to pleasure. This stands out in contrast to the way medievalists perceived curiosity; for Augustine it was aimless, and for Aquinas it was more like sloth, having little direction. By the seventeenth century, curiosity came to be associated with a focused and disciplined activity. If curiosity *seemed* useless, then it was praised as being disinterested pursuit of knowledge for its own sake.

Curiosity had an obsessive quality, so that the 'annals of seventeenth century natural philosophy abound with stories of interrupted meals, forsaken guests, and missed bedtimes as observers dropped everything to devote themselves to a fleeting, fascinating phenomenon'.[3] The scientist Francis Bacon helped to cement the link between wonder and curiosity. Yet he also had a passion for application, using the results of science for the purposes of human ends. He believed that those wonders in the natural world considered monstrous should be occasions for learning; for him such natural wonders were creative possibilities for the future. In other words, while Aristotle believed that the so-called 'errors' of nature destroyed order, for Francis Bacon they became ways of inspiring new orderings in things. He also believed that scientists needed to study and ultimately control such variations in the natural world, rather than ignore them. Descartes took a step further again, suggesting that the difference between human technology and the natural world made by God was simply one of scale and complexity. He also distinguished between wonder as admiration that could be used for good effect, and other forms of wonder that were more stupefying. Wonder as admiration promoted inquiry, but wonder as astonishment might dull the intellect. But, by the end of the seventeenth century, the difference between technology and nature became obvious once again through Hooke's discovery using a microscope that the point of a needle was not smooth, as it appeared to the naked eye, but ragged and imperfect. A more limited sense of unity between technology and nature came through seeing the natural world as also 'the art' of God, God as the divine artisan or craftsman. Naturalists of this period were also commonly ministers in the Church, taking delight in finding order and regularity in the natural world as evidence for divine artisanship.

The story of what wonder means is not over yet. By the eighteenth century, the link between curiosity and wonder became severed once again. Wonder persisted at the turn of the eighteenth century as a means to promote praise, rather than intensify further exploration. For Robert Boyle wonder was due to God, so that all natural objects became examples of divine handiwork. Others sought to find wonder in the regularities and laws of the natural world, rather than in novelty or rarity. But such attempts failed, for by the middle of the century 'wonder had sunk among the learned to the level of the gawk'.[4] In other words, wonder came to be linked with the ignorant, rather than the sophisticated. Curiosity, on the other hand, which Augustine had once associated with lust and pride, now gained an elevated status.[5] Wonder changed from being an emotion at one time associated with awed reverence to that of a dull stupor.[6] Daston and Park suggest that 'the wonder that had once been hailed as the philosophical passion par excellence was by 1750 the hallmark of the ignorant and barbarous. On the other hand, curiosity, for centuries reviled as a form of lust or pride, became the badge of the disinterested and dedicated scientist.'[7] In this way, wonder became 'the ruling passion of the vulgar mob, rather than that of the philosophical elite'.[8]

Such negative connotations of wonder persisted in the Enlightenment period. Scientists who used the term of wonder were suspected of enthusiasm, while those who spoke about wonder in the context of religion were thought to be superstitious. In this period the capacity grew for invention, discovery, venture capital and conquest – all were themes that stressed active pursuits rather than contemplative virtues. Wonder as that which arrests the gaze leads nowhere, according to this view, and is therefore more likely to be associated with childhood, or the uneducated, or even lunatics in Western culture.[9] The counter-Enlightenment view, perhaps still with us today, is that wonder can reclaim a lost childhood, snuffed out by reasoning. But this view still accepts, in common with the Enlightenment, the dichotomy of reason and the marvellous. The marvellous seemed to be detached from the safe, the seemly and the possible. This also had its influence in theology, so that 'the quiet exit of demons in respectable theology coincides in time and corresponds in structure almost exactly with the disappearance of the preternatural in respectable natural philosophy'.[10] Such wonders might entertain, but they could also terrify. Hence wonders could elicit a wide range of responses, and with it the potent feeling of wonder. But wonder as an experience remains in the work of serious theologians, even if they generally no longer consider that the spiritual realm is populated with demons and angels. Søren Kierkegaard, for example, claimed that 'the expression of wonder is worship. And wonder is an ambiguous state of mind which comprises fear and bliss. Worship therefore is mingled fear and bliss all at once.'[11]

Does, as Daston and Park suggest, the odour of the popular still cling to wonder? Certainly, contemporary scientists writing in academic scientific journals would be loath to be found admitting to such emotions. Yet, once scientists write in book form for a more popular audience, then wonder once more comes back into the vocabulary. But should wonder be slighted in this way? The philosopher Immanuel Kant translated wonder into the sublime, and in this way saw it as an instrument of reason. Contemporary philosophers may also follow suit. In the first place wonder, like terror, is an experience that is capable of transforming us because it touches us at the core of our being. But wonder refers to something more than just inner experience. The philosopher Jerome Miller, for example, believes that the experience of wonder is not simply about subjective emotion, but refers to objective events in the world that would otherwise pass over our attention.[12] He suggests that, philosophically speaking, wonder means that everything is questionable. In this way 'as wonderers, we do make a breakthrough to the beyond, but we do so by becoming aware of it in its very character as beyond us – as transcending what is given to us'.[13] More significantly, perhaps, it is the unknown that breaks through to us, not we who break through to the unknown. In this way he suggests that to be fully rational is to surrender unconditionally to the throe of wonder, a letting go of control. This is the opposite of mastery over the unknown, which promises to provide a way out of the uncomfortable feeling that we have when engulfed by wonder. The temptation is to allow the unknown to be colonised, taken over by what is familiar to us. The difference from the familiar never emerges in this scenario. The alternative is to let the other be in the sense of allowing oneself to be vulnerable to its difference and overcome by it. In this way, 'to enter the unknown as unknown instead of trying to colonise it requires our approaching it in a spirit of meekness and voluntary poverty'.[14] This leads to inquiry without a method, for a fixed method would mean that our maps are already set up in advance. He realises that this is a radical suggestion; some might suggest it is 'the death of thought itself'. But 'To the one who undergoes it, who awakens in wonder to the other in its otherness, it seems like the birth of genuine thinking. To the one who is in the throe of this turn, it is like dying and being born at the same time.'[15] Such language is already familiar to the mystic and the theologian. But remarkably enough, Miller is writing purely from the point of view of secular philosophy. He has therefore taken wonder out of the realm of popular, and placed it at the heart of the way he sees serious thinking should take place. One might even give a similar account to the experience of great discoveries in science, a realisation of a reality beyond oneself which seems to beckon the scientist to acknowledge its truth. Miller has, in a sense, retrieved the notion of wonder at the start of philosophy, but also taken it further, and made wonder the core of philosophical method. It also allows for the possibility of the sacred, for according to this view, everything is questionable, including a more contemporary philosophical rejection of religious experience. Scientists may, therefore, begin to bring back the notion of wonder as positive, especially those who are interested in the dialogue with religion. Marco Bersanelli and Mario Gargantini have illustrated the importance of wonder as implicit among key scientists, both historically and among contemporary writers.[16]

WHAT IS WISDOM?

If wonder might have seemed somewhat elusive in its varied interpretations through history, wisdom has an even greater variation in pedigree. Almost all interpreters believe that it is in the nature of wisdom to be difficult to define or pin down with any precision. Yet we can identify various strands in order to bring some clarity, even while being conscious that too tight a definition undermines the very nature of wisdom itself. We can also understand wisdom from a number of different perspectives.[17] Nancey Murphy argues for a hierarchical understanding of wisdom, so that physical reality is at the base, followed by organic, then mental, then social, then moral and then religious or spiritual.[18] There is an obvious sense in which this hierarchy is true, in that if there were no physical reality there would be no organic reality, and so on, towards the final layer. Yet there are also serious drawbacks in this approach. In the first place, it presumes that the 'top' spiritual layer is only reached when humanity emerges. This would seem to deny the possibility of spiritual wisdom in nature other than humanity. In addition, the hierarchy creates the unfortunate impression of elevating humanity to a place that would be denied by the wisdom traditions themselves; wisdom is the acceptance of how much I do not know, it is always a search and is never complete. I would much prefer, therefore, to speak of different *facets of wisdom*, rather than wisdom as layered reality. I am also going to deliberately start with a philosophical discussion of wisdom, for it is capable of putting into perspective those facets of wisdom that are more narrowly defined, in other words, those arising out of contemporary science.

Philosophy means, literally, love of wisdom. The aim of ancient philosophers was the contemplation of life as a whole. They knew nothing of the specialisation and fragmentation that is characteristic of modern ways of knowing. Wisdom, according to this view, is the active pursuit of knowledge as a whole, rather than simply a collection of information. As well as this, the ancient philosophers believed that understanding *goodness* must be at the heart of all knowledge. Modern science, with its bent towards particular discoveries, has lost this contemplative stance, always straining ahead after the new, instead of reflecting more deeply on what is there already and working out the implications.[19] Perhaps, in the light of our discussion on wonder, we might say that much of science has become addicted to those forms of wonder or wisdom that are tethered to the leash of science. Early science was part of philosophy, but Enlightenment thinking eventually crystallised the split of scientific knowledge from wisdom. Although philosophers like Immanuel Kant tried to overcome this crisis by making moral knowledge a separate sphere from natural knowledge, it actually accentuated the problem. For now philosophy could confine itself to the moral, leaving the natural realm to the natural sciences.[20] Eventually philosophy took the form that we are more familiar with today, that is asking questions about why we know what we know.

Theology, no less than science, has also transformed itself. Ancient philosophy considered questions about God, but theology eventually became restricted to the moral realm, and more recently it has become a way of thinking about religion in isolation from the rest of life. Nicholas Maxwell calls for a philosophy of wisdom, the recovery of the tradition of Socrates in philosophy, so that it is concerned with life, rather than just knowledge.[21] He believes that such a shift will allow us to concentrate on problems that are really important for life and living.

The link between wisdom and life is also a key characteristic of the way wisdom was perceived in the Hebrew Bible. Wisdom could be learned in the family, or through education, or through oral traditions passed down from one generation to the next. Since wisdom is about reflection on daily life, one Hebrew scholar has called the wisdom literature the *tree of life*.[22] These ancient writers believed that wisdom had to do with a certain quality of life that could be passed on through education. The concerns of wisdom were political, administrative and moral. Wisdom writers hoped to instil the lessons learnt from human experience to other members of society, so that they would reach agreement in decision-making. The language of wisdom was poetic and full of images in order to instil particular points. Wisdom writers also assumed that God exists, and so they emphasised that the beginning of wisdom is the fear of the Lord. Hence, anyone who denied that God exists was a fool, not capable of knowing wisdom. Wisdom teaching was more open to different interpretations as to the right path to follow, and in this sense was far less rigid than the law, which was much more precise in its instructions. Wisdom facilitates the freedom of choice of the individual and the community, but such choices are those that are ultimately directed towards a good end. The fool fails to anticipate the outcomes of their decisions in terms of the consequences, but there may also be room for different decisions depending on particular circumstances. Wisdom enables such decisions where there are complex factors at work and where simple application of laws would be difficult. Wisdom teaching, in other words, left some of the responsibility for decision-making to the individuals concerned; it encouraged active reflection, rather than passive reception of rules. Wisdom writers also encouraged the building up of particular traits of character that display moral virtues and moral integrity. But wisdom writers were also aware of the dangers of such concentration on living a life of virtue, for it could lead to a false sense that righteous action is always and inevitably rewarded. Qoheleth, the author of Ecclesiastes, challenges conventional wisdom by pointing to the inevitability of death and suffering, regardless of the energy we put into seeking to live a life of virtue.

The idea in the Hebrew literature that wisdom is something of value that can be passed down from one generation to the next implies that wisdom is rooted in human experience of life, rather than an emergent property of our biological nature. Yet the story may not be as simple as this implies, for the very capacity to think in complex ways is also dependent on particular patterns of brain function that may have an evolutionary component. Jeffrey Schloss, for example, examines evolutionary perspectives on wisdom in the light of current evolutionary theories.[23] Of course, as with any more empirical study, it is important to be clear what exactly is meant by wisdom if we are to trace its evolutionary history. Drawing on the discussion in the Hebrew biblical literature, he proposes that:

> Wisdom is living in a way that corresponds to how things are. It is not mere knowledge, nor is it mere moral admonition, but it involves deep insight into the functioning, meaning and purpose of existence along with the ability to

discern how to live correspondingly, that is, in accord with the way things are.[24]

This seems to me to be as useful a working definition as that related to human behaviour and morality. Yet he is also concerned with tracing how such behaviour might have arisen in the first place through a close study of evolutionary history. Theories drawing on Darwin's understanding of natural selection stated that the variation that we find within species contributes to different fitness to a given environment. Those that are most suited to the environment will reproduce more offspring and pass on these genes to the next generation. But the matter is not quite as simple as it seems. For many evolutionary biologists believe that some variation does not arise through selective pressure, but is neutral in this respect, arising through other processes such as genetic drift, where traits appear that are incidental to the selection process. Sociobiologists have traditionally wanted to interpret human behaviour in terms of Darwinian theory, so that human behaviours have to be explained in terms of reproductive fitness.[25] The account of how wisdom might contribute to such fitness would require somewhat convoluted reasoning, though it might be possible to argue that the possession of wisdom raises esteem in a community, and so leads to more reproductive success. The fact that many of those who were thought to have wisdom were celibate makes this explanation unlikely. At the other end of the scale are those who believe that complex cognitive functions arise more incidentally from other cognitive traits which may be selected for their adaptive value. Such complex cognitive functions would include things like human morality and religion.[26]

Related to the story of adaptation is how far such traits are also genetically determined. Most scientists would deny that cultural variation is directly linked to genetic change. However, they do debate how far culture might in some sense be *constrained* by genetic variation. They also debate how far tendencies in human behaviour might be a result of genetic adaptations and the extent to which variations in cognition and social behaviour are related to differences in genetic make up. The most 'conservative' sociobiologists like E. O. Wilson argue that culture is kept on a 'genetic leash'. Richard Dawkins, among others, suggests that there is no direct tie up between genes and culture. In other words, the leash may 'break', but biology will also influence behaviour. He proposes a dual inheritance system through 'memes' (cultural practices or ideas) and genes. Social scientists, on the other hand, are more likely to argue that human cultural behaviour is largely independent of human biology.

The ability to learn reflects the possibility of being able to respond to new and challenging situations with immediate effect. It goes without saying that novelty in learning does not require genetic change. It therefore represents a secondary level that is distinct from the primary genetic level. Human culture may represent a third layer above this learning capacity that is not constrained by genetics, even though it may be influenced by it.[27] Practices such as celibacy could be accounted for in this account, and so in this respect at least it is preferable to the rigid coupling between genetics and culture proposed by E. O. Wilson and others. The difficulty here is that there is no guarantee that cultural innovations will be adaptive; some might even be positively hostile towards our biological functioning. Jeffrey Schloss suggests that wisdom might represent a means of filtering out those cultural innovations so that they are in tune with the needs of our more basic biological natures.[28] In other words, it represents a fourth layer that is capable, where necessary, of challenging cultural norms. He is aware of important questions that remain even in this case, for example, how have human cognitive abilities become apparently free from the constraints of genetic evolution? There are also more fundamental difficulties with dual models of inheritance, for these presuppose a radical split between our material and biological natures. They certainly do not seem to fit well with wisdom. Schloss also suggests that the need for wisdom may have arisen initially through a requirement for more integrative ways of thinking that could serve to resolve conflict. It may also serve to highlight the dangers of self-deception. Finally, it could be required in those instances where there is rapid cultural innovation.

Of course, those who see wisdom more in terms of psychological function are more inclined to define wisdom in a rather different way. While intelligence relates to underlying capacity for higher cognitive functions, according to Warren Brown wisdom 'is a term used to denote markedly successful problem-solving ability, particularly in personal and social domains, in the face of complexity, subtlety, novelty, and/or uncertainty'.[29] Scientists can identify examples of neurological malfunction where the ability to understand new or complex information is missing. In this respect human wisdom presupposes adequate brain function. Yet, this is not the same as saying that wisdom can be *reduced* to such function, although understanding how the capacity of wisdom might relate to other higher cognitive functions such as consciousness is also important.

Although human wisdom might be traced through evolutionary history to human capacity for seeing things in holistic ways, drawing on human experience, the precise *content* of what wisdom might entail is also important if we are to move beyond mere generalities. Thomas Aquinas saw wisdom as one of the three intellectual virtues of speculative reason, the other two being understanding and science. Wisdom was about the relationship between everything and everything else, including God. He also distinguished wisdom from prudence, or practical wisdom, which was skill in the art of deliberating, judging and acting. This distinction is important in order to clarify different facets of wisdom, even if generally the one considered wise is capable of both speculative and practical reasoning.

The Hebrew Bible also included not just individual and community aspects of wisdom, but cosmic aspects as well. This means that the writers perceived wisdom as being present right at the start of creation, rather than simply added on as a layer to human experience. Theological reflection on wisdom takes this image still further, attributing wisdom to God as well as the cosmos. In other words, I am suggesting that we need to move away from thinking of wisdom just in terms of human beings, even though it makes sense to start with this discussion. Why? Because gaining wisdom is about the close study of all creatures, not just human beings. It is a way of thinking not just about human culture, but an integration of those insights into alternative cultures, such as that found in social animals.

RELATING WONDER AND WISDOM

My proposal in this book is that wonder helps to set the agenda for wisdom. Wonder might arise from the close study of perfectly ordinary events in life. Or it may, as I indicated earlier, arise from more unusual occurrences that might even seem frightening or threatening. If philosophy is simply open to the throes of wonder without wisdom it is in danger of becoming unhinged, especially where wonders are sought for their own sake. Wisdom reminds wonder of the human capacity for self-deception. Wonder reminds wisdom that there is always more to learn, that the search for wisdom is never at an end. Both wonder and wisdom are efforts of what I would term the *imaginative intellect*, that is reason and imagination are brought together in a creative and synergistic way. There is also another human faculty related to imagination that I suggest brings wonder and wisdom together which is particularly relevant, and this is the faculty of *paying attention*. Both experiences require close attention to details, to the other, in a way that allows wonder and wisdom to flourish. While wonder may be the first movement, wisdom is notably the second in paying attention, though the search for wisdom itself may lead to another layer of wondering that some might prefer to call beauty. What are we paying attention to?

Aristotle believed that philosophical wisdom was intuitive reason combined with scientific knowledge. Is intuition really possible or is it simply a reflection of cultural prejudices? If we take this stance then all we are left with is a pragmatic basis for wisdom as practical advice in difficult circumstances. Yet some sense of the reality of truth is necessary in order to begin the task of seeking wisdom. There is a paradox here, in that while the existence of truth is not in dispute, once someone believes that they possess the truth, then wisdom ceases. According to Miller, 'wonder is the hinge that turns my attention away from the immediately present towards what can only be known through questioning' and 'wonder is the hinge that opens up the absolute future ... a future that is so different from the now that opening the door to it is really the beginning of a new world'.[30] In other words, wonder opens up wisdom not just to reflection on the natural world, though it certainly includes this, but by doing so opens another dimension, namely the dimension of the transcendent. Wonder beckons us to a future that does not simply emerge out of our origin, but towards a new future that can best be described in theological language. This is why discussions about wisdom that concentrate simply on the scientific analysis of wisdom may fall flat, for by their nature they are forced to relinquish any aspect of teleology from their discussion. Wisdom in the throe of wonder, on the other hand, challenges science to recognise its proper place in the scheme of knowledge, as one facet of knowing among others.

Yet how can we understand what it means to pay attention? Simone Weil believed that the capacity to pay attention 'taken to its highest degree, is the same thing as prayer. It presupposes faith and love.'[31] Moreover, she suggests that 'extreme attention is what constitutes the creative faculty in man and the only extreme attention is religious. The amount of creative genius in any period is strictly in proportion to the amount of extreme attention and thus of authentic religion in that period.'[32] She also warns against the type of attention that either fixes simply on the problem, or shows a wrongful dependence on the object of our efforts. In this way, 'It is only effort without desire (not attached to an object) which infallibly contains a reward.'[33] In other words, an obsessive attachment to wisdom is bound to fail, as the Hebrew writers were well aware. It comes, rather, indirectly, and it is an attention that is so full that the 'I' disappears. She also suggested that we are indifferent to good and evil, but that the good wins through as we pay attention to both. This capacity for the good to shine through is, she suggests, the work of grace. Paying attention to God – or to a lesser degree anything that is truly beautiful – makes certain things impossible for us. By this she means that humanity is capable of holding together the true, the beautiful and the good by paying attention to God.

Such discourse on paying attention implies that if we merely restrict our gaze to the natural world then this will limit our appreciation and, in this sense, both our wonder and wisdom will be diminished accordingly. This book begins, therefore, with reflections on our capacity to wonder, but it is wonder arising out of the experience of the natural world around us, including that described by contemporary cosmology. The first chapter focuses on debates about the origin of the cosmos in theories about the Big Bang and the wonder arising from these discoveries. We will also explore the origin of life in the far-flung history of the earth, for this, too, is tied up with its cosmological history. The second chapter deals with life on earth; specifically with the way naturalists have come to appreciate the natural diversity on earth as charged with wonder.

While some have seen religious connotations in such natural expressions of wonder, both in the cosmos and life, others have not. Is it helpful to think of God as designer or not? The third chapter on natural wisdom takes this idea further, through an exploration of evolutionary convergence and design in the natural world. How might this mesh with theological understanding of natural wisdom? The fourth chapter deals more specifically with the human capacity for wisdom, taking up some of the issues explored in this introduction, and asking different questions about human identity in the light of the earlier chapters.

The fifth chapter is unashamedly theological in its focus, exploring the notion of God as wisdom and asking what this means. Even those who believe religion is a human projection have to admit that the way God's wisdom is articulated will shape an ideal of wisdom towards which human aspirations are drawn. The sixth chapter turns on the paradox at the heart of the Christian Gospel accounts, namely that the crucified one is also demonstrating God's wisdom. What is this foolishness to the Greeks? Certainly, understanding divine wisdom as in some sense crucified means that we no longer need to think of suffering as detached from God's concern. How far and to what extent is evolutionary suffering caught up in the suffering of Christ?

The seventh chapter returns once more to the theme of wonder. Yet this time it is wonder chastened in the light of the wisdom of God and the wisdom of the cross. The journey now takes on a more explicit mystical element, but it is a mysticism that is ultimately grounded in earthly reality, rather than separated from it. It is a journey that those readers of the book who are believers may care to follow. Those who are not may look on with bemused attention. Yet it is my hope that if the arguments for wonder and paying attention presented here are convincing, then it is also a journey that cannot be ignored. The opening of wonder has presented a space in which it becomes possible once again to speak in religious and spiritual terms.

Linda Woodhead believes that there is a mirror relationship between organised religion and spirituality, with the latter now dominating with the demise of formal religion.[34] Of course, this model only really works well in Europe, where secularisation has taken a strong hold, but spirituality prevails. I am less convinced that it is true for North America, for here spirituality seems to exist alongside a powerful and well-churched majority. The model of spirituality that I am proposing here would appeal to both types of religious experience. Those attracted to more alternative religious traditions will find the affirmation of nature's worth reassuring. On the other hand, those attracted to organised religion will find that there is a place for a recovery of the classics, and an inclusion of insights from both the Eastern and the Western religious traditions. African spirituality, with its love of life, will also connect with the themes developed in this book.

I am conscious that covering so many themes in one book will in all probability irritate some more academic readers. Yet it is my contention that without such a broad overview much closer analysis becomes somewhat futile, for it represents a capitulation to that loss of wisdom, understood as integrated knowledge. Such loss has now been ignored, as it is no longer recognised as such. By beginning with wonder I hope to fuel the desire for that more holistic wisdom once again. As Mary Midgley has claimed:

> First comes the initial gazing, the vision which conveys the point to the whole. The vision is in no way just a means to practical involvement, but itself an essential aspect of the goal. On it the seeker's spirit feeds, and without it that spirit would starve.[35]

ONE

WONDERFUL WORLD

WHERE HAVE WE come from? Or more particularly, how did our earth come into being? Questions that search back into the origin of the universe and the origin of life on this earth are both scientific and religious. Scientific, as they help to tell us more about the physical processes that led to the early evolution of the earth, and religious, as they raise profound questions about meaning. Contemporary physicists have shaken up the way we think about the world. Physical reality is no longer simply that described by Newton's laws but, through quantum physics and relativity theory, matter seems less bounded than we once thought. The experience of wonder comes to the surface as deeper observations give way to greater understanding, and a greater sense of unknowing even at the heart of physical reality.

WONDER AT THE UNIVERSE'S ORIGIN

Is ancient cosmology obsolete following the Copernican revolution, which showed that the earth was not the centre of the solar system, and the solar system was not the centre of the universe? While the early cosmologists thought that the universe began some 8–10,000 years ago, current estimates make it closer to 12–15 billion years ago. Although one might think that cosmology in antiquity would make no sense in the light of the explosion in scientific knowledge over the last half century, surprisingly enough there are still repeated themes that have ancient roots.[1] Aristotle favoured the idea that natural laws

[19]

sustained the universe in a steady state; his opponents believed that the universe began as a single point. Plato rejected the idea that an increase in complexity arose through fundamental properties of nature. Another ancient philosopher, Anaxagoras, believed that the universe would continue to expand indefinitely, but Epicurus believed that it would cease to expand once it reached a given density. We are more accustomed to believing that their understanding of the world was completely mistaken, and certainly they were wrong in thinking that humankind and the earth were at the centre of the universe. But the idea lingers on in a different guise in the Anthropic Principle, which we will come back to again in more detail below. Also, although the ancients believed that the universe had an 'edge', more recent discussion also speaks of the 'edge' of space around black holes, for example. These historical studies are important as it makes us aware that cosmology then, as today, is a construct of human intelligence, even if we have far more sophisticated scientific means of trying to work out which theory is the most likely.

Fred Hoyle, writing as recently as the 1950s, believed in the Aristotelian idea that the universe existed in a steady state, and introduced the phrase 'Big Bang' to denote the alternative theory that he rejected. The Big Bang theory proposed that the universe began from a 'Singularity', but it is not so much an explosion out into space, for at the start there was neither space nor time. Hoyle's opponents gradually won the argument, as if the Big Bang theory was right, there should be an 'afterglow' of that radiance still in the universe.[2] Scientists first discovered this afterglow, 2.7 degrees above absolute zero, in 1965, with more support for this ever since. The first millisecond of the Big Bang is beyond the reach of any physical laws. The material here would be denser than any atomic nucleus. After the first millisecond the physics is known. According to this theory the first few minutes in the origin of the universe were searing hot, so hot that nuclear fusion took place. But if it had stayed hot for too long, then everything would have turned to iron, an atom with the most tightly bound nucleus. About a quarter of the hydrogen turned to helium, with some deuterium (or heavy isotope of hydrogen) present. Remarkably, it took thousands of years to cool down to the temperature equivalent to that of our sun! In this time, the universe became dark until the first stars were formed. Galaxies of stars gradually formed from an amorphous mass of material about one billion years after the start, or 'Singularity', but crucially it was material that had different initial densities. Many large stars later died by exploding as 'supernova', and the explosive force for these comes from neutrinos, which are 'ghostly entities', largely devoid of any physical properties.[3] Scientists believe that our own solar system arose from one of these supernova explosions.

The stars that we see around us are not the sum total of matter in outer space, for astronomers have calculated that the gravity would be insufficient to keep galaxies together. Instead, much of the material in the universe is made up of 'dark matter'. Astronomers have found clouds of cold hydrogen circling beyond visible stars, and other astronomical evidence for dark matter comes from gravity making light bend as it passes dark material. Much of this dark matter is thought to pass through ordinary material with no interaction with it at all. More important perhaps, calculations suggest that the bulk of the material in the universe consists of this elusive dark matter. The level of initial gravitational instability after the Big Bang, also known as 'Q', is also crucial. In the formation of stars, gravity first pulls gas into clumps of dark matter, and then it cools and condenses into drops that form stars. If the figure of Q were much smaller that 10^{-5} then clumps of galaxies could never have formed. The gravity would not have retained the gas that then led to the formation of stars. A smooth universe would 'remain forever dark and featureless'.[4] On the other hand, if the relative gravitational densities were more exaggerated, if the initial conditions led to a 'rougher' universe, with Q much larger than 10^{-5}, then much larger galaxies would form, and they would either collapse into vast black holes, or be in solar systems where stars would be packed so close together that any planets would be hit by passing stars.

There are, of course, some black holes even in the present universe, where gravity takes over other forces, so that even light cannot escape. Our galaxy has relatively fewer black holes compared with other known galaxies; some black holes have the equivalent density of a billion suns![5] Space and time around the edge of the black holes are distorted, but the distortion is not a mystery, as it follows Einstein's theory of general relativity.[6] The very centre of the black hole corresponds to the initial Singularity, in that in this region beyond space/time the physics of the process is unknown.

Astronomers have also speculated that there might be an extra energy repulsive force in space which works in the opposite direction to gravity. Einstein called this force 'lambda'. Although he misjudged its size, scientists now think that lambda comes from a vacuum effect, but it is one that 'pushes', rather than 'pulls', and it is uncertain why it was once a dominant force but now is only very feeble and barely detectable. The total amount of mass and energy in the universe is thought to be about 66 per cent of this so called 'dark energy', 30 per cent dark matter, mentioned above, and a mere 4 per cent which includes stars, glowing gas and so on. This echoes an ancient concept of a 'fifth essence', which plays no immediate role in stars or galaxies, but drove the rapid expansion of the universe at its earliest stages.

One of the difficulties encountered in the Big Bang theory is that predicted by quantum physics which follows Heisenberg's uncertainty principle. This principle states that you cannot measure with any accuracy both the location and energy of a given particle. But another puzzle for theoretical physics is why there are any atoms at all, for one might have expected all matter and corresponding antimatter to cancel out, leaving just a glow of radiation in the form of gamma rays before stars had the chance to form. One of the reasons for the existence of anything at all is that there is slightly more matter compared with anti-matter, a staggering one part in a billion.

WONDERFULLY DESIGNED UNIVERSE?

Our galaxy is one of over 50 billion galaxies in the universe, each with billions and billions of stars. Overall, astronomers are staggered by the orderliness of the universe, for there are literally endless ways in which it might have been different.[7] It might, for example, have had no physical laws, or these laws might have been incoherently jumbled together, or laws might not have consistently applied over time. As mentioned above, it might have been featureless, or devoid of matter or motion. It might have changed its state in random or complicated ways. The universe is also ordered in a very special way between simple orderliness, as found in a crystal structure, and random complexity. The complexity has arisen gradually from what appeared to be an unstructured beginning. Another feature is the general coherence in the natural world that has allowed the universe to be the way it is. For example, the force of gravity and the mechanical and thermodynamic properties of hydrogen gas create large numbers of balls of gas which then trigger nuclear reactions. If these reactions had been more intensive, this would have led to black holes being formed. Instead, stable stars emerged in the beginning. Another remarkable feature is the uniformity of nature expressed in physical laws; the cosmological principle, for example, the magnetic moment on an electron, is the same throughout the known universe. The physical laws were not sufficient to account for life; favourable environments were also a basic requirement. Paul Davies is less concerned about 'parochial' issues of life on earth, for he, like many others, recognises that unless the laws of physics met certain requirements, life would never have got started.[8] He suggests that he is 'convinced that the universe could have been otherwise ... There could have been different laws. The fact that we live in the kind of universe we do is very suggestive that not only has a selection been made, but a rather intelligent selection. There are so many remarkable features of the laws that characterise this universe that it's very suggestive of something like design or meaning or purpose.'[9]

The force of gravity, the heat-generating nuclear reactions in the stars and the sun, the mass of the electron, its electric charge and the violence of the Big Bang – all these features were 'just right' in order to favour existence and ultimately the emergence of life.[10]

The physical processes in operation seem, remarkably, to be 'fine-tuned' so that life could emerge. Why should this be so? The link between the human ability to observe and the laws and conditions of the universe is called the Anthropic Principle. The Weak Anthropic Principle (WAP) states that we can only observe the universe from places and times where intelligent life can exist.[11] This can predict under what conditions intelligent life would be possible, in the manner suggested by Paul Davies above. If scientists could define the initial conditions and physical laws, then it would be possible to predict where other life might exist in the universe. This kind of approach gives the range of physical laws where life might come to be, but does not fix the values exactly. But the unsolved question is why is there life anywhere at all? The Strong Anthropic Principle (SAP) goes further and claims that intelligent life *must* exist in the universe as a necessity. One reason is that quantum theory requires an 'observer', so without an observer quantum theory would be impossible. Yet not all scientists are convinced that quantum theory does have such an absolute requirement for an observer. In addition, we could ask why such a form of quantum mechanics, with its observer, is really crucial for the universe. The WAP is, therefore, the most convincing version of the Anthropic Principle.

Scientists have discovered in all kinds of other ways that the properties of our solar system are just right for life to have formed.[12] Carbon is an exceptional element as it forms up to 10 million different compounds. Biologically active organic compounds need water as well as a certain range of temperature in order to be active. Around 4 billion years ago, when life first was thought to have formed, the rotation speed of the earth meant that there were five-hour day cycles. Over millennia this has lengthened to the 24-hour day that we experience now. The braking effect is a result of tides caused by the gravity that the sun exerts on the earth. If the earth had been closer to the sun, then tidal braking would have been such that it would have led to a 'locked' state after a few billion years, where only one side of the planet would see the sun. Venus is almost completely locked; each 'day' is equivalent to 117 of our days. The sun is one of the G stars, which have 12 billion years of life. If it had been an M star, for example, with 300 billion years of life, then within the habitable zone for temperature the planet would have been permanently locked. If this is taken into account, then only four times 10^{17} stars have an earth-like planet in a continuously habitable zone. This might seem like a large number, but it is a very small proportion given that there are an estimated over 50 billion *galaxies* in the universe, each with a billion stars or more. The earth itself is thought to have formed around 4.56 billion years ago, with initial asteroid impacts vaporising the oceans and preventing any water formation up to 4.2 billion years ago. It took a relatively short period of time in the cosmic scale, a mere 300 million years, for life to begin from pre-biotic stage to earliest microbial life forms. Some estimate an even shorter time, especially if a cataclysmic event evaporated all the water in the oceans some 3.9 million years ago.

There are some scientists, like Martin Rees and Peter Atkins, who dismiss the idea that the universe is in some sense tuned in for 'life'. They argue that there are additional universes, even billions and billions of universes, but the physical conditions suited for life just happened to take place in our universe, and perhaps others as well. This places contingency at the heart of the coincidence of all the physical laws coming together in a manner fit for life. For them, it just happened apparently by accident that this universe had all the pre-conditions met.[13] Atkins believes that the idea that God somehow worked in order to render all the physical constants just right for life is too complex a notion. He suggests that 'it is much simpler to believe that universes just tumble into being (whatever that means) and if one of them happens to have the right mix, then life will take hold in it. This is intrinsically much simpler than a designed universe.'[14] He believes that those who hold to the existence of God on other grounds, and then postulate a 'designed' universe are 'deluding themselves'. Paul Davies, on the other hand, persists in pressing the question as to why there is intelligent life at all, arguing that the way the universe is ordered gives meaning to human existence. He then adds further that 'Our existence as sentient beings

in the universe links in to the basic laws of physics in a meaning-
ful way. And I think that provides human beings, in a modest but
important way, with some sort of deeper significance to their
lives.'[15] He believes that the idea of a designer God is consistent
with physics, but it would be a matter of 'personal taste' whether
one wanted to subscribe to this view.

Is the theistic claim the best possible explanation? What if
more evidence accumulated for Atkins' view? Would this necessarily be fatal for theism? What if the laws of the universe have
changed and become selected over time, as some cosmologists
have suggested lately? Like Bob Russell, I am much more wary
than some Christian physicists seem to be about claiming that the
universe is deliberately designed.[16]

In the next chapter, we will see how early natural historians
believed that they had found evidence for God's handiwork in the
intricate design of living forms, only to be quashed relatively soon
afterwards by Charles Darwin's explanation in terms of a theory
of evolution by natural selection. While I have my doubts about
the adequacy of a multi-universe explanation, there are likely to
be yet more alternative, 'natural' explanations which have not yet
reached human consciousness. In addition, we can ask what kind
of God does a designer God portray? Is God simply a brilliant
mathematician? Perhaps God fixed the initial conditions? Or was
God in the energy of the earliest beginnings? But this brings back
the spectre of deism, an absent God, and certainly not the personal
God known through Christian traditions of spirituality. But there
may be another way of wondering about the evolution of the
universe that opens up a deeper sense of mystery, which I will
return to below.

WONDER AT THE ORIGIN OF LIFE

What is known so far? The Russian scientist Aleksandr Oparin
(1894–1980) reasoned that organic compounds arose from
spontaneous reactions taking place early in the earth's history.
Carbon, released from chemical bonds with metals, would react
with hydrogen and ammonia to form hydrocarbons and cyanide.

Although at one time scientists thought that asteroids from space might have sourced 'life' by providing amino acids, this theory has become far less popular following experimental laboratory work trying to synthesise life artificially. Stanley Miller, working in Chicago in the 1950s, gave experimental support to this idea by synthesising a mixture of amino acids from a mixture of reducing gases (gases that add hydrogen or electrons in chemical reactions), consisting of hydrogen, ammonia and methane. Crucially, he realised that the process needed an energy source, which he achieved by subjecting the gases to an electric charge. Miller synthesised over 30 amino acids, as well as some cyanide. Later researchers found that cyanide, in sufficient concentration and in the right conditions, would produce adenine, one of the building blocks of nucleic acids. There are competing theories about how life could have assembled from these building blocks. Some scientists believe that proto-metabolic processes happened first, prior to the formation of information-carrying molecules, in other words, genes. Others argue that reactions took place on iron–sulphur supports. In all probability all kinds of 'trials' took place simultaneously, with the newly fragile life systems being much more unstable than even the microscopic life that we know about today.

Thomas Cech, a chemist who won the Nobel Prize for his work, argued that the molecular basis for the very start of life resides in ribonucleic acid (RNA), rather than deoxyribonucleic acid, or DNA, which goes to make up the human genome. RNA is particularly important as it can act both as an enzyme, speeding up chemical reactions, and as an information carrier, passing down replicated information from one generation to the next. What is life according to Cech?[17] He believes that life requires information flow, hence its secret is storing and using vital information. Information superimposed on certain states of matter or energy distinguishes life from non-life. Is this enough? In addition, for life to exist there needs to be a membrane envelope in order to enclose the reactions and thus to form primitive cellular structure, though the definitions of what 'life' is are as numerous as definitions of what 'nature' is. Most definitions also include the ideas of self-organisation, self-replication and dynamic evolution.

Chemists have come close to spontaneous reproduction of RNA, though there are still plenty of gaps. Some scientists believe that it is virtually impossible to replicate the early conditions of earth, and that the sequence of events or 'coincidences' required according to some theories are about as credible as explanation by miracle, so outside the boundaries of recognisable science. If scientists eventually solve these puzzles, then this implies that self-assembly of molecules fit for life happened relatively spontaneously, so that Cech can say that while it is likely that a number of different chemical forms of life emerged, the one that persisted is the one that we have now.

How far does it make sense to speak of the 'purposeful' emergence of life from its earliest pre-life beginnings? The gradual increase in complexity in the timeline of life is an ongoing feature of life as it unfolds which defies full explanation. Some scientists believe that it is a property of physical matter itself, that differences in energy states drive the increase in complexity, rather than any intrinsic tendency towards order. This has the advantage of being compatible with the increase in entropy according to the second law of thermodynamics. However, they would refrain from suggesting that such directional behaviour expresses an intentional purpose or teleology.[18] Yet I think that energy states cannot account for the emergence of complexity, for such energy states seem to express a tautology, that is, for life to physically subsist and not break the laws of thermodynamics, then some shift in energy states is inevitable. A more important question is, *why* does the process move towards energy states that then allow the emergence of complexity? Physical answers seem appropriate at one level of explanation only.

The timeline of the way life emerged from its earliest origins goes something like this.[19] About 5 or 6 billion years ago, a supernova named Tiamat exploded in the Orion arm of our galaxy, the Milky Way. Our solar system was formed from the debris of that explosion, and the earth needed about a billion years to cool down before it reached a temperature fit for life to exist. Between 4.2 and 3.9 billion years ago the earliest life forms were prokaryotes (that is, bacteria or cyanobacteria, which are organisms lacking organelles). By 3.9 billion years ago a descendant, known as *promethio*, had developed the capacity for photosynthesis using the energy of the sun to sustain life and fix carbon from atmospheric carbon dioxide. This transformed the gaseous composition of the earth from an abiotic to an oxygen-rich atmosphere. By 2.5 billion years ago, a descendant of *promethio* named *prospero* had developed the ability to survive the high concentrations of oxygen that had built up, through developing the capacity for respiration. By 2 billion years ago eukaryotes formed, that is creatures that had a nucleus separated from the rest of the cell. By 700–500 million years ago multicellular creatures and fish emerged, along with the appearance of the capacity to reproduce sexually. This led to an explosion of life forms in the Cambrian period. By 400 million years ago life first emerged from the sea, then 235 million years ago there were the first dinosaurs, with mammals appearing soon after this. Two hundred and ten million years ago the original continent floating in the ocean broke up, leading to more speciation and diversification. Ninety million years ago flowering plants became dominant, and in the same period monkeys and apes first appeared. Just 4 million years ago the first hominid ancestors appeared, with *Homo habilis* some 2.8 million years ago, *Homo erectus* 2.4–1.0 million years ago, and *Homo sapiens* some 300,000–200,000 years ago.

The timeline is an estimate only, as it becomes ever more difficult to assess the further back into history one goes. The final stages of evolution may be even more complicated than this, as shown by the recent discovery of a new human species. In October 2004, scientists named *Homo floresiensis*, a new species of human discovered on the island of Flores in Indonesia.[20] This human species, nicknamed '*hobbits*', was smaller than its ancestor, *Homo erectus*, and adapted to the particular living conditions of its island home. The species was only a metre tall as adults and, according to the fossil record, lived on the island from 70,000 to 18,000 years ago.[21] The point is that these humans were alive well into the time when *Homo sapiens* existed. Hence, mythological stories about yetis or other human-like creatures coexisting with humans may be based on the real possibility of their existence at some time in human history. The discovery certainly challenges a naive view that humans emerged from the primates in a linear way, with each emerging *Homo* species developing new powers and characteristics.

WONDER AT THE MYSTERY

The emergence of the universe fit for life, against all the seeming alternatives, the emergence of life itself and its increase in complexity are enough to leave even the casual reader spellbound in wonder. As space exploration began to show the living planet earth, a jewel in what seems a lifeless galaxy, the feeling of wonder became ever stronger. Even the sheer size of the universe and its myriad galaxies mean that 'one does not have to be especially spiritual to experience awe at the infinity of galaxies we can see in the night sky'.[22] The start of the whole process of the universe, as expressed in the Singularity, goes beyond what physical science can reasonably describe. The rationalist assumption that reality is entirely knowable no longer applies in this case, so that at the limits of this reason 'we encounter a mystery, not in terms of gaps to be filled, but as the ineluctable mysteriousness of the whole thing'.[23] In other words, wonder is at the mystery of what is known to be mystery, rather than simply the unknown. As the universe unfolds, the increase in complexity leads to ever more dimensions that are known to be beyond the tools of physical science, as in, for example, black holes. Has this opened up the idea of mystery as a positive experience, rather than simply the gaps in our knowledge that need to be filled?

As long as cosmological mystery is seen in this light, that is, in the light of wonder, then I think it can be positive. Less positive would be the idea that somehow God is here, but not in the rest of the process. Yet the creativity of the unfolding process of the evolution of the universe, where there are continuously creative acts ongoing throughout the history of time, would imply an image of God as one who is present throughout the process, rather than simply at the beginning, or where physical laws no longer seem to hold. For the cosmologist the ultimate wonder is that things exist at all, that we have being, so that Claus Brockelman can say that 'wonder seems not so much an explanation or a hypothesis about how or why things work as they do, but an experiential noticing or awareness of their being as opposed to their non-being'.

In wonder, we 'pay attention' to the reality itself, to existence, generating a feeling of inclusion.[24] The wonder is both at why we exist, that we are formed of atoms from the stars, but also at the amazing scope and scale of the space and time which exists in our universe. Wonder is a natural reaction to the exuberant and astonishing power of things to be, to exist at all. What follows this experience of wonder? Is the response now one of gratitude? But if we feel a sense of gratitude, is it towards the anonymous universe, or towards God, as the ground of all Being? Certainly, if we feel a religious sense of awe at the mystery of the vast universe and our own small existence, then this is just as likely to promote fear as much as the more comforting sense of gratitude.

CREATION AND CHAOS

How far do the classical notions of God as Creator fit with the wonder that has opened up in the field of physics and cosmology? Many scientists who are trained as physicists are attracted to the idea of process thought, the philosophy that depends on the thought of Alfred North Whitehead. Certainly, the Jesuit priest and scientist Pierre Teilhard de Chardin anticipated these ideas, holding out a view of reality that argued in favour of psychic energy pervading the universe, from its very beginning. While Paul Davies suggests that human connectivity with the laws of the universe provides meaning, the ultimate fate of the universe from such physical laws is one of purposelessness and eventual collapse, either through cooling or heat death of the universe.

Teilhard was one of the first Christian writers to explicitly counter such pessimistic views of scientific eschatology with his

Christian vision. Although, as a palaeontologist, he was primarily concerned with the way life evolved, he was also aware of the burgeoning interest in the origin of the universe. He wanted to counter the mood of pessimism about the fate of the universe with a Christian vision of the future which also took into account the scientific cosmology of his day. He believed that materialistic explanations of the universe which explored physical energy and anticipated the ultimate death of the material universe, failed to see matter from the 'inside', a spiritual energy that he named 'psychical' energy.[25] He also believed that finding the unity of matter in universal physical reality expresses a unity from below. Instead, he argued for a unity from above, arising from increasing levels of complexity. Above all, he insisted that we keep spiritual and physical energy together, rather than separate them as in much of the Christian tradition, and indeed in the tradition of science. This psychical energy as *tangential* energy led to independence and as *radial* energy led to a movement towards complexity. How does this energy reserve tie in with the second law of thermodynamics? In order to get round this, Teilhard proposed that spiritual energy used only an infinitesimal fraction of physical energy. He also envisaged the direction of evolution in ever-higher stages, first the appearance of living things, biogenesis; second the appearance of self-consciousness in humans, noogenesis; and third the appearance of Christ, Christogenesis. He believed that the universe could only fulfil its goal when it reaches the Omega point, where Christ is all in all.

Process philosophy, like Teilhard, supposes a form of psychical energy in all things. However, process thought finds it more difficult to envisage the significance of Christ, or indeed the meaning of the Trinity. Instead, in process thought God is thought of as having two poles, with one pole as the contingent God emerging from the stuff of the universe. God, in process thought, lures and persuades the universe towards ever-greater complexity and beauty. Although God's two-poled nature prevents process thought equating God with the universe in its entirety, it is difficult to recognise the place of Christ in process thought. John Haught's approach to cosmology and creation is one of the more successful versions of process theology which manages to avoid this danger to some extent.[26] For him, immutability in God means that God is faithful to the divine promise. The universe, as discovered by science, may lead to wonder, but Haught believes that it can also lead to a profound sense of cosmic homelessness. He argues, instead, that the natural world is not so much a threat, as a harbinger of cosmic promise. He believes that we can come to see meaning in the way the universe is by seeing humanity as part of the story of the cosmos, an adventurous story prepared to take risks, so that viewed over the long term eventually life, mind and human culture come into existence.

The idea of the universe as a *story* becomes more explicit in the work of writers such as Brian Swimme and Thomas Berry, who were both heavily influenced by Teilhard.[27] Of course, it is easy to be more optimistic when the first half of the story is explored, that is our universal history up until now, rather than focus on more pessimistic scientific projections into the future! In the first place, they argue that we need to see the second law of thermodynamics, the law that claims the universe is breaking down in order, alongside another law, that of cosmogenesis. The Cosmogenetic Principle, a development of Einstein's Cosmological Principle, states that every part of the universe is the same and the dynamics of evolution are the same as well. The suns of spiral galaxies, for example, all evolve through stages, eventually collapsing into a burnt-out dwarf or black hole. Atoms, such as hydrogen atoms, are the same throughout the universe. More specifically, 'If we consider an indifferent universe in either a chaotic or an equilibrium state, the chances that a galactic structure will evolve within a billion years are negligible.'[28]

Differentiation, self-organisation and communion, they argue, structure the ordering capacity of cosmogenesis. Differentiation refers to the immense diversity of the universe, and it is a diversity that continues to develop. Also, the interactions that govern the newly emerging stars or galaxies are different from those that govern elementary particles and so on. Such differentiation also applies within one group as well, pointing to individual uniqueness. Such uniqueness implies 'an inexhaustible fecundity at the root of reality'.[29] The structure of the universe unfolds through its capacity for self-organisation, or *autopoiesis*, pointing to creativity in matter itself. Stars or galaxies have the capacity for organisation. All of this seems to point to the interior capacity for self-manifestation. What is the relationship between this and later, more obvious, capacities for complexity in living organisms?

Swimme and Berry suggest that the universe has a latent capacity within it, in a mysterious way hidden as dimensions of emptiness, even though we see a radical overall movement from molten rocks to mammalian consciousness. This is a more convincing way of expressing Teilhard's idea of psychic energy, as the latter gives the incorrect impression that matter is in some sense sentient, even though this is not what he intended. The unfolding of the universe also includes, they believe, the idea of *communion*, of interconnectedness of everything with everything else. Our sun, for example, emerged out of the creativity of former beings to which it was interconnected. Such interconnectedness continues in more obvious ways once life appears on the planet, but it is there even at the beginning of time. Like Haught, the authors want their readers to enter into the earth story and feel the power of its exuberant expression. The response to this sense of wonder is celebration, which is, for them, deeply connected with a sense of the sacred. The drumbeat of Native American Indians is somehow resonant with the pulse and rhythm of the universe. They argue that we need to weave into our religious celebrations those significant moments of the universe story, without which life could never have come to be.

While such an optimistic vision might inspire us to care more deeply about this fragile earth in which humans find themselves, how far is it realistic in the face of other elements within this wonderful world that actually give a deep sense of foreboding? John Polkinghorne writes about the end of the world in terms that hold onto the tenets of Christian faith.[30] Global warming and climate change are happening at an unprecedented rate, and given the time that the human species has lived on this planet, there seems no guarantee that human life will continue indefinitely.

It is here that reflections on creation and chaos are helpful, for chaos theory helps to unravel how far and to what extent the earth can become destabilised. In particular, has the traditional view of creation out of nothing, upheld in the Christian tradition, now become obsolete?[31] While the biblical account in Genesis is not intended to be a scientific document, I think that the theme of order out of chaos is worth taking seriously in a theology of creation. I am, however, reluctant to equate the initial primordial beginning of the Big Bang with the Genesis text, however suggestive this seems.[32] Why? If we read Genesis this way, then we might be tempted to equate other aspects of the Genesis story with science, so that, for example, Adam and Eve become real persons, which clearly they are not, and we move onto the slippery slope of a creationist view of science, where the text competes in some sense with scientific knowledge.

However, the more general idea that God orders in some sense through holding back chaotic forces is worth exploring a little further.[33] It is also worth reconsidering the notion of creation out of nothing in the light of contemporary science. It strikes me that, given the potency of that early event, the pre-existing energy operating outside physical laws and the immense capacity of that event for creativity, then even if we no longer hold to a literal view of creation *out of nothing*, the question still remains as to *where* the latent energy and matter that sparked off the Big Bang and subsequent creation came from in the first place. A Christian view of God as Creator would see God as creatively working within such a process and beyond it to the evolution of the cosmos, but it is not possible to say with any assurance whether God created this early starting material or not. If God simply created the material and then left the universe to itself in the Big Bang, this is as unsatisfying theologically as seeing God as somehow guiding the unfolding evolution of the pre-existing matter of the universe. Yet to posit God as in some sense just providing the ordering of chaos in creative evolution creates as many problems as it solves. Suffering and disorder simply emerge from these leftover chaotic elements. Such a view neatly removes the tricky questions about the apparent 'darker' sides of the universe, including eventually the suffering present in the evolved life of planet earth. Our fear latent in wonder at the universe story becomes a real fear, a fear of chaos seemingly outside the Providence of God. But if this is an explanation of evil, then it is hard to envisage how God in Christ could ever overcome these forces of evil by becoming human and suffering in Christ, especially if we hold to a trinitarian concept of God acting in creation.

The Genesis story also speaks of God creating the serpent, which implies that God's Providence is *over* evil, rather than outside it. If we follow the biblical account of God ordering chaos in the book of Genesis, then chaos is not outside the Providence of God, but under such Providence. If we view chaos as a force opposed to creativity in God, this resonates with a dualistic account of cosmology according to the Gnostic tradition of a battle of good and evil, even if now that dualism is expressed in terms of energy states, rather than matter as such. My preference would be to see chaos as that which is permitted by God to exist in order to enable creation to be itself. The fear implicit in the wonder at this wonderful world can come to rest in contemplation of who God is, a God who ultimately expresses Love and Goodness. It is God as Wisdom, working with natural wisdom, which permits chaos to exist, as will become clearer in chapters that follow.

CONCLUSIONS

I have outlined in this chapter the scientific story of the origin of the universe and the origin of life within planet earth. This story on its own gives a profound feeling of awe and wonder at the amazing set of coincidences that seemed to accompany the evolution of the universe. Physicists are astonished not only at the way the ordered nature of galaxy upon galaxy has gradually unfolded in the history of the universe, but also at why there is anything at all. It is way beyond human imagination to consider that the very stuff of the billions upon billions of stars is but a fraction of dark matter and dark energy, which in themselves are but a billionth of the initial matter that self-annihilated into gamma rays at the primordial flaring forth into being. Coincidences upon coincidences mount with the emergence of life, so that early fledgling life appeared as if by some cosmic accident. Humanity itself becomes just an afterthought in the vast history of time; even our Neolithic ancestors are close to us in terms of the universe story.

But science points to a bleak future, which mixes celebratory wonder at life's diversity in all its cosmological and biological expression with profound fear and dread. How do we deal with this ambiguity? Do we put more emphasis on the genesis of the universe, recognising that the second law of thermodynamics may not be the last word? Or do we try to look closer into the meaning of God as Creator, seeking to understand what such a Creator God means in the light of contemporary science? While the concept of creation out of nothing is implausible if taken to mean that the universe had no matter at the beginning, the question still remains as to where this matter has come from. Perhaps we will never know the answer, but reflection on the Genesis text can remind us that God is a God who brings order in the midst of chaos, and works through that chaos. While the idea of evil as emerging from left-over chaos is appealing in its explanatory power, it sets up a dualism in energies that is reminiscent of Gnostic tendencies in early Christian centuries. But before we move deeper into the question of how God might act as Creator of all that is, we need to consider more carefully in the next few chapters the wonderful nature of life itself in all its diversity and marvellous fecundity.

TWO

WONDERFUL LIFE

IN WHAT SENSE might living nature serve to inspire the emotion of wonder, and how is this connected with religious experience? The tradition of natural history, seeing nature in a way that paid attention to her variety and intricacy, was a prelude to evolutionary theories that tried to explain that diversity. Did Darwin's theory of natural selection destroy a sense of wonder, or lead to its reinterpretation or even enhancement? Given the chequered history of what wonder means, is it now becoming respectable for scientists to admit to this emotion?[1] Is wonder at the origin of life and of human life dented by the experiments designed to trace these origins in naturalistic terms? Is wonder compatible with religious experience of the transcendent? It is to these questions that we shall now turn, comparing the wonderful as far as biologists are concerned, with that experienced by physicists exploring the origin of the earth through cosmology in the previous chapter.

WONDER IN NATURAL HISTORY

Arguably, the tradition of being both a priest and a naturalist began from the beginning of Christianity, following the inspiration of the early Celtic saints, Augustine's and Aquinas' appreciation of the beauty of nature, and the example of Francis of Assisi, often called the patron saint of ecology. Augustine reinforced the idea of wonder as that associated with the holy. Francis of Assisi did not view the natural world through a modern scientific lens, or have any knowledge of ecology as such,

yet the early saints used poetry to express something un-
fathomable about human feelings towards the natural world.
Francis can, though, be rightfully called a 'nature mystic', for he
wove his encounter with other creatures into the depth of his
religious experience. He felt, in other words, a sense of mystical
rapture when taking delight in the creatures around him. He even
moved a stage further, according to legends about Francis, bringing creatures into conversation about spiritual matters, and
perhaps even inviting creatures to praise God in the *Canticle to
the Brother Sun*.[2] This Canticle gave special attention to the
sources of life on earth – water, sun, air, fire, weather and so on
as expressing an interdependence that is arguably modern – for
such sources are vitally needed for the sustaining of life, as
environmentalists now fully recognise. His notion of 'creatures'
was not like our modern usage, but blended the organic and
inorganic worlds, personifying the sun, moon, water, winds and
so on. Biographers speak of Francis's experience with creatures
leading to profound 'joy, love, rapture and adoration of the
divine in creation', often 'filled with a wonderful and ineffable
joy' in his encounters with the natural world (p.96). He knew, in
a profound sense, what it was to 'pay attention' to creatures, so
much so that he reached the heights of mystical ecstasy. In the
words of one scholar, his 'responsiveness to the beauty of the
environment was so great, his joyful openness to it so boundless,
that he experienced mystical ecstasy while contemplating a
flower' (p.145). His *Sermon to the Birds* shows that he believed
humanity needed to take an interest in the needs of creatures in
their own right, leading to a sense of kinship with all creatures.
Yet it would be incorrect to see the Franciscan movement as a
counter-movement to other strands in Christianity that encouraged exploitation of the natural world. Rather, drawing especially
on biblical sources, he affirmed the goodness of creation in a context where many felt a deep ambivalence. His life and vision
inspired artistic expressions that could themselves become
sources of wonder and appreciation for the natural world. Use of
more 'scientific' information about wonder tended to draw on
cosmology, and though there were some medieval bestiaries that

made direct links between observations about the natural world and religious belief, the knowledge of the behaviour of animals was scant (p.94).

William Turner (1508–1568) is arguably the beginning of a particularly English tradition of being both a parson and a naturalist.[3] Turner, like other naturalists of his time, believed that the natural world could be a vehicle for expressing praise due to the Creator. These naturalists were, perhaps, less 'innocent' in their appreciation of the natural world compared with Francis of Assisi, yet they shared the characteristic of wanting to pay close attention to it, believing that by so doing they would learn more about the God whom they worshipped as Creator of all that is. John Ray (1627–1705) took the observation of the natural world a step further, and arguably paved the way for the first botanical systematic classification scheme. His wonder at the natural world gave him a deep joy that could be said to be akin to that of Francis before him. For example, in his preface to the *Catalogue of the Plants of the Cambridge Area*, the first *English Flora*, published in 1660, he declared that: 'First I was fascinated and absorbed by the rich spectacle of the meadows in spring time; then I was filled with wonder and delight at the marvellous shape, colour and structure of individual plants.'[4] Yet he went on to make further discoveries of considerable scientific value. His paper 'On the Seeds of Plants' separated monocotyledons from dicotyledons, one of the major divisions in the plant kingdom. Though he did not fully appreciate the significance of this division, it marked an important step forward.[5] He also published a second paper, 'On the Specific Differences in Plants', that recognised that structure and morphology should be used in plant classification, rather than other characteristics, such as petal colour. In addition, perhaps anticipating Darwin's later theories, he recognised that 'nature' always produces species that fall into particular types, with some that are difficult to classify, as they are intermediate in their characteristics.[6]

The eighteenth century carried on and intensified a more serious study of plant and animal life, but the tradition of wonder remained, though more as that which emerges out of such study, rather than independent of it. By the dawn of the nineteenth century natural history had become a clearly established science. The priests and naturalists were in their heyday in the nineteenth century, and supported natural history societies and field clubs. John Stevens Henslow (1796–1861), for example, was a priest and naturalist who became Darwin's teacher and friend. The variety and diversity of creation pointed to a divine Creator, though Darwin himself struggled to explain his discoveries through the traditional explanations of individual creation. Although he was thought to be a somewhat indifferent student, he was, out of school hours, deeply interested in natural history and collecting all sorts of life forms. Darwin's revolutionary ideas began to crystallise while he was on an epic journey round the world in a warship, *HMS Beagle*, given the mission to draw up maps of places likely to be of significance in future conquests. Reading his journal one can sense the 'wonder, the doubt and hesitation, and the slowly mounting certainties that led Darwin along the path to the evolving universe'.[7] His discoveries on the Galapagos Islands were particularly important for the development of his theory. Here he found species that were unique to the islands, and in addition, they varied from one island to the next, having characteristics that fitted them perfectly to their environment. On 13 September 1835, an entry to his journal after his arrival at the Galapagos Islands reads: 'The natural history is very remarkable: it seems to be a little world within itself, the greater number of its inhabitants, both vegetable and animal, being found nowhere else.' For example, he discovered 26 different species of land birds, including 13 species of finches, still known as Darwin's Finches, which displayed a range of beak characteristics from thick beaks to fine and warbler-like beaks on different islands. He struggled to understand why this was the case. At times his journal shows that he asked himself why the Creator would have made so many different varieties in such a small area. Yet at other times he used more obviously evolutionary language, speaking in terms of adaptation and fitness for a particular environment. His sense of wonder was not diminished by such discoveries, but enhanced by them.

Of course, the choice that Darwin had to make, and one that those who follow after him still have to make, is whether giving a natural explanation for such diversity is inimical to religious faith or not. His theory of natural selection, which developed more fully after he returned from his trip, was remarkably simple. It stated that there is variation in the natural world and that those individuals that are best suited to the environment survive the longest and consequently produce the most offspring. Lamarck's alternative scientific idea was that the environment directly influences key characteristics that are then passed down to the next generation. Both views, it could be said, challenge the notion of divine design, but while for Lamarck the key influence seemed to come from outside the individual species, for Darwin it was built into the natural variation existing in given populations. Darwin had some scientific allies. In 1858 A. R. Wallace sent Darwin a paper on the survival of the fittest, but Wallace was prepared to admit that Darwin had reached his ideas much earlier, soon after his return from his trip aboard *HMS Beagle* in 1844. Both Darwin and Wallace read a joint paper to the Linnean Society in 1858. While the publication of Darwin's *Origin of Species* in 1865 led to some controversy in scientific terms, by the end of the century few doubted its efficacy as an explanatory hypothesis.[8]

It is hardly surprising that his ideas sparked intense religious controversy, accustomed as many were to viewing the work of the Creator in terms of intervention for the emergence of variety in the natural world. There were some, like Henry Baker Tristram (1822–1906), Canon of Durham Cathedral, who warmly welcomed his ideas, even after his first joint paper with Wallace at the Linnean Society. Philip Henry Gosse (1810–88), a fellow naturalist with Darwin, strongly objected to Darwin's ideas. For him, the wonders of the world are necessarily connected with the infinite mind of God, expressed as God's wisdom.[9] He held on to his ideas about individual creation by an omnipotent Deity in spite of mounting evidence to the contrary. Yet, over time, more Christians became convinced that the scriptural basis for defending the notion of divine individual creation of species was itself open to doubt. Biblical exegesis exposed the early story of

Genesis as not so much a text about the material origin of the world, but more a way of thinking about the involvement of God in human history, including its material origins. The early creation story, including that of the Fall of humanity should be interpreted as mythology, rather than literal truth. This way of interpreting the Bible freed many Christians from the fear that accepting Darwinism was equivalent to atheism in the way Philip Gosse contended.

WONDER IN ECOLOGY

After Darwin we might have expected the tradition of wonder to be diminished; the image of nature as red in tooth and claw, alongside the rhetoric of competition, might seem to be opposed or even hostile to the tradition of wonder, especially the kind of wonder that leads to awe and reverence, rather than fear and ambivalence. Yet if we read accounts of even hard-boiled Darwinians like E. O. Wilson, it is clear that his experience of the natural world is one that is pregnant with wonder. Wilson contends that humans possess an innate tendency to focus on life and life-like processes, such tendency he calls *biophilia*.[10] He argues that modern biology is a genuinely new way of looking at the world, which happens to be in tune with this tendency. Yet it is through such a search that he believes we discover the core of wonder, for it is still replete with this capacity due to the rich abundance of life in comparison with our relative ignorance of it. Accordingly:

> Now to the very heart of wonder. Because species diversity was created prior to humanity, and because we evolved within it, we have never fathomed its limits. As a consequence, the living world is the natural domain of the most restless and paradoxical part of the human spirit. Our sense of wonder grows exponentially. The greater the knowledge, the deeper the mystery and the more we seek knowledge to create new mystery. (p.10)

Wilson wonders at simple biological facts, such as that a handful of soil and litter is home to hundreds of insects, nematode worms and other larger creatures, alongside a million fungi and 10 billion bacteria. Other amazing facts include the genetic information required for one particular insect – if printed as standard size letters it would stretch over a thousand miles. So much does wonder impinge on his thinking that for Wilson the mysteries of nature are analogous to a 'magic well' (p.19). He is aware, as are many other biologists, that 90 per cent of species are not even named, and species are disappearing faster than they can be identified. Amidst a tropical rainforest, the sheer diversity of life is such that there are literally thousands of undiscovered species, with the number of discoveries per investigator greater than anywhere else in the world. Leaf-cutting ants also give pause for wonderment, since no other animals have evolved to turn fresh leaf cuttings into a garden suitable for fungi cultivation. He observes that 'they consume more vegetation than any other group of animals, including the more abundant forms of caterpillars, grasshoppers, birds and mammals' (p.33). The mother queen ant is the size of a newborn mouse! But he has no sense that the ant colony is conscious in the way humans are, for he admits, rather, that 'I never see the colony as anything more than an organic machine' (p.36). But this mechanistic philosophy does not prevent him from having a sense of wonder, for 'because biology sweeps the full range of space and time, there will be more discussion renewing the sense of wonder at each step of research' (p.54). Every biologist might say Amen to that.

But now Wilson has to account for why we wonder in the first place, and it is here that his biological philosophy begins to show its cracks. Commenting on Einstein's creative genius he suggests that mathematics and beauty play on the human brain's limbic system in such a way as to promote further survival and enhanced reproduction (p.61). But I, for one, have not noticed any particular reproductive prowess amongst mathematicians. If anything, mathematicians find it harder to be socially accepted in a community, in spite of their search for beauty, and by association, wonder, in their formulations! His mechanistic and materialistic understanding of the way the mind works and his interpretation of human behaviour as simply programmed through biological cues borders on the offensive. He struggles, for example, to explain why human beings continue to feel awe and veneration towards serpents, claiming that 'the mind is primed to act emotionally to the sight of snakes, not just to fear them, but to be aroused and absorbed by their details, to weave stories about them' (p.86). It is hardly surprising that philosophers, such as Mary Midgley, find plenty of ammunition against these ideas.[11]

Wilson tries, somewhat unsuccessfully, to argue his case for a coming together of the natural sciences and the humanities. Could forms of wonder unite both enterprises? He compares science in its earliest stages to poetry, again, hinting at the way the humanities and sciences are related: 'But where scientists aim for a generalising formula to which special cases are obedient, seeking unifying natural laws, artists invent special cases immediately. They transmit forms of knowledge in which the knower himself is revealed' (p.62). Yet we should take this seeming accommodation of the value of the humanities with a pinch of salt. For Wilson becomes more and more vocal about his real intention behind relating the natural sciences with the humanities, and that is for the humanities to be absorbed by the sciences and reconfigured through the latter's knowledge.[12] While other philosophers might agree with him that there needs to be a gradual self-disclosure between science and the humanities, he does the cause of biology a disservice by using rhetorical devices such as the language of conquest and imperialism which imply an underlying arrogance on his part in favour of biological knowledge.[13] One might add that this imperialising tendency is opposed to the very wonder that he is trying to foster among fledgling ecologists, which accounts for opposition to his views both inside and outside the scientific community. One of the reasons that he may have thought that this strategy would work is that it appeals to both group instincts and inter-group hostility, as according to him territorial expansion is 'an epigenetic rule'.[14] The fact that his strategy failed shows that human nature is not operative in the way he assumed.

Rachel Carson, a biologist writing in the era before E. O. Wilson developed his sociobiology, argued passionately for the wondrous appreciation of the natural world. However, this appreciation did not lead her to announce the tyranny of biology over all other forms of knowledge in the manner expressed through Wilson's rhetoric. Rather, it came from a more fundamental anxiety about what might happen to the world if humans continued to despoil the environment through their activities. Although Wilson used the language of wonder to express how he felt personally in his forays in natural history, he appealed to baser aspects of human nature as a basis for environmental protection. The natural world was valuable for its instrumental use to humans, so that it could be viewed as an untapped source of new pharmaceuticals, crops, fibres, and so on.[15] Carson also believed that the despoliation of nature was not in humanity's best interest, and one of her best-known works was *Silent Spring*.[16] However, she also tried to foster a deeper appreciation of the natural world by using the language of wonder to describe what she saw. Carson's life and work have inspired many to care more deeply about nature in such a way that is accessible even to the youngest minds.[17] She believed that wonder is a prelude for care for the earth, and in this her views are directly contradictory to those of Wilson. For example, she claimed that: 'The more clearly we focus our attention on the wonders and realities of the world about us, the less taste we shall have for destruction,' and 'A child's world is fresh and new and beautiful, full of wonder and excitement. It is to our misfortune that for most of us that clear eyed vision, that true instinct for what is beautiful and awe inspiring is dimmed and even lost when we reach adulthood.'[18] Was she adhering to a return to romantic views about wonder – wonder as a rediscovery of a lost childhood? Certainly, where such romanticism means a total rejection of science it fails to convince. Yet Carson was hinting at something profound about the pattern of wondering, namely that it allows us to pay attention to what is, and in this sense comes closer to the religious instinct in wonder that Wilson only partially expressed.

Annie Dillard is a novelist who has also written about natural history, but more from the perspective of a popular writer, rather than a biologist as such. Yet her detailed accounts of the observation of nature in *Pilgrim at Tinker Creek* (1974) enabled many to integrate their understanding of nature as a biological process with religious concepts. The creeks were, for her, a source of mystery at 'the uncertainty of vision, the horror of the fixed, the dissolution of the present, the intricacy of beauty, the pressure of fecundity, the elusiveness of the free and the flawed nature of perfection'.[19] She is more conscious than some, perhaps, of the cruelty embedded in the natural world, a cruelty that is profoundly disturbing. She describes in graphic detail how a giant water bug first injected a frog with poisonous enzymes, which liquidised its brain and muscles, and then proceeded to suck out the contents reduced to a juice, leaving only the shell of a frog skin to float away in the water (p.6). Yet she is also aware of beauty and grace (by which she seems to mean gracefulness, rather than theological grace) and wonder at the sight of sharks appearing and disappearing along a sea horizon, so much that 'The sight held awesome wonders: power and beauty, grace tangled in a rapture with violence' (p.8). She is prepared to admit that:

> ... we don't know what is going on here. If these tremendous events are random combinations of matter run amok, the yield of billions of monkeys at millions of typewriters, then what is it in us, hammered out of these same typewriters, that they ignite? We don't know. Our life is a faint tracing on the surface of mystery, like the idle curved tunnels of leaf miners on the face of a leaf. (pp.8–9)

Such wonderment leads to a sense of meaninglessness, one that is free floating as it is decoupled from a wider sense of human purpose, or purpose in creation. Hence, even while she is prepared to admit that behaviourist philosophy such as that expounded by Wilson and others falls short, she is left not knowing what to do with that wonderment. Yet the challenge remains, for who can account for the seeming extravagance in the evolutionary

? She contrasts the mechanistic view that evolution in
ınstrosity, mixed with profusion, is a result of random
vents 'careening blindly from nowhere to nowhere, or,
following Julian of Norwich, a view that God has been intricately
involved in every creative act, so nothing can be amiss'
(pp.177–8). Yet she hesitates to adopt the latter view, as she
believes Julian is frankly wrong that 'nothing is amiss', so her
alternative is to suggest that somehow human beings are the ones
that are 'amiss' in feeling the way that they do. Yet might there
not be a way of incorporating the shadow aspects of the natural
world into a theological perspective? Dillard seems to assume
that this is impossible, but she seems to have opted for wonder
divorced from theological wisdom, and thereby rejected religious
truth as being an option.

Richard Dawkins is one of the most vitriolic in his attack on
religious ideas and concepts as viable ways of knowing. For him,
the most authentic form of wonder follows from science, with
religious views rejected *tout court*. Yet, if we probe a little into
the way he thinks about life, it becomes clear that his version of
wondering is close to the poetic. He suggests, for example, that:

> The impulses to awe, reverence and wonder which led Blake
> to mysticism (and lesser figures to paranormal superstition,
> as we shall see) are precisely those that lead others to
> science. Our interpretation is different but what excites us is
> the same. The mystic is content to bask in the wonder and
> revel in the mystery that we were not 'meant' to understand.
> The scientist feels the same wonder but is restless, not con-
> tent, recognises the mystery as profound, then adds, 'But we
> are working on it.'[20]

In other words, wonder is the gateway into scientific exploration for the scientist, an 'unweaving' of the rainbow. We might
also distinguish another source of wonder that comes indirectly
through scientific explanation, a wonder at the mysteries revealed
by science. The examples from natural history and cosmology
discussed in an earlier chapter show both kinds of wonder. There

is the immediate impact, but then it is deepened further by scientific investigation. He assumes, incorrectly, that direct and indirect sources of wonder are incompatible with religious belief, a view that is naive both historically and philosophically.[21] Dawkins is correct to suggest that it would be equally naive to assume, as did some of the poets, that scientific investigation automatically destroyed a sense of wonder.

However, neither Dawkins nor his critics have really paid sufficient attention to the way wonder was historically rejected as being incompatible with reasonable science following the Enlightenment. Hence, it is easy to find historical examples that imply wonder is incompatible or compatible with science, depending on the historical period under review. Perhaps we might say that Dawkins contributes to a new accommodation of wonder with science in a way that is positive. Or does wonder still carry popularist connotations, writing as Dawkins does with a popular audience in view? In admitting to the emotion of wonder through science Dawkins presents us with a rather different view of the way science works, compared to highly critical approaches that have implied that scientific observation has taken over and replaced narrative descriptions of reality.[22]

The question that now needs to be asked is whether the kind of wonder that Dawkins speaks of is like a smokescreen, hiding a deeper cultural agenda that wants to exclude other ways of thinking about reality. A charitable view would argue that Dawkins has, by promoting wonder in science, served a good purpose for inspiring others to take up the mantle of scientific research and enjoy its secrets. The practice of science is certainly not as sterile as those outside the community sometimes presume. It is still a profoundly human exercise, bringing with it the rich feelings of wonder that Dawkins recognises himself. On the other hand, his evangelism for science and scientific wonders is indicative that it has fulfilled a religious role. In this respect it borders on the fears expressed by those early scientists who were Christians, such as Robert Boyle, that a focus on wonder in itself usurps human and divine authority over nature. For him wonder could only be directed to God, anything else amounts to idolatry. It is clear that, as far as Dawkins is concerned, religious ways of thinking are now virtually redundant, even though his expression of the value of wonder is remarkably religious in tone. It is also clear that E. O. Wilson believed that only biological paradigms are now of use culturally, and so should be adopted by the humanities as well. On the other hand it is no longer possible to return to naivety, to a lost innocence about the world prior to the Enlightenment.

In order for wonder to find its proper place in science it needs to include direct and indirect experiences of wonder, but also be connected, at least obliquely, with a third aspect of wonder, that which acknowledges the transcendent. Barbara McClintock is a good example of a biologist who was ready to admit, at least in private, of her capacity to wonder and its link with transcendent realities. She undermines Dawkins' thesis of the incompatibility of religious experience with science and scientific wonder in one fell swoop. She was also a recipient eventually of a Nobel Prize for Medicine for her work in genetics, but it was work ahead of its time, marking her out to be a woman of remarkable ingenuity and originality. Her biographer, Evelyn Fox Keller, stresses that McClintock made her discoveries by developing a 'feeling for the organism', synthesising the twentieth-century focus on experiment with a naturalist's emphasis on observation.[23] The naturalists' approach is one that dwells particularly on the variety and complexity of organisms. Rushing too fast to an explanation through science using the scientific method may lead to other important questions about the natural world being missed. In other words, scientific study should be seen in its proper context as an expression of part of reality. McClintock was also prepared to admit that the mysticism of the East inspired her thinking, but these aspects of her world remained obscured from scientific scrutiny and did not surface in her scientific papers. Dawkins, and to some extent E. O. Wilson, lacks the humility of great scientists such as Barbara McClintock, who had the vision to 'think outside the box'.

Pierre Teilhard de Chardin was another scientist who found the wonder he experienced in science compatible with religious wonder. His work in palaeontology gave him scientific acclaim, especially his work on human origins. Like Barbara McClintock, he was attracted to Eastern forms of spirituality, but he wrote out of a committed Christian faith and he was an ordained priest in the Jesuit Order. Unlike McClintock, he also wrote about his experiences in a way that synthesised a commitment to evolutionary theories in science with a religious understanding of reality. As a mystic he was open about the experiences of wonder that he encountered, arising out of a deep sense of the presence of God in the whole of created reality. He describes his book, *The Divine Milieu*, as an attempt 'to give distinct expression to my wonder and amazement', and even just before the end of his life he confessed that 'the wonder and passion will still be there, undimmed'.[24] The divine milieu is that which interpenetrates the whole of existence, so that for him 'all creatures, every one of them, cannot be considered in their nature and action without the same reality being found in their most interior being – like sunlight in the fragments of a broken mirror – one beneath its multiplicity, unattainable beneath its proximity, spiritual beneath its materiality.'[25] Our minds cannot comprehend what is desirable in the natural world without going back to the source. God as the source of the very structure of things compels us to look at what is really desirable in the natural world, and this can lead to 'inexhaustible wonders which the divine milieu has in store for us' (p.76). Teilhard invites his readers to 'plunge into God', and become established in the divine milieu, so he can add:

> ... the fact that all the external springs of the world should be coordinated and harmonized at that privileged point is not the only marvel. By a complementary marvel, those who abandon themselves to the divine milieu feel it clearly directs and vastly expands their interior powers with a sureness which enables them to avoid, like child's play, the numerous reefs on which mystical ardour has so often foundered. (p.77)

In other words, for him the wonderful was at its most intense in spiritual mystical experience, but it was one rooted in and arising out of deep contemplation of the universe and life on earth, rather than in detachment from it. Is this pantheism? Teilhard hotly denies this charge, for 'pantheism seduces us by its vistas of perfect universal union' but, if true, it would lead to a type of 'unconsciousness', for all elements would vanish in the God so created. By contrast, for Teilhard, 'God ... pushes to its furthest possible limit the differentiation among the creatures he concentrates within himself' (p.77). There is both a sense of unity, which McClintock also speaks about, but equally a profound sense of human distinctiveness.

WONDER AT HUMAN ORIGINS

Teilhard's religious views supported the concept of hominisation, the view that with the appearance of humankind something distinctive took place in evolutionary terms. Teilhard assumed that self-reflexivity is characteristic of *Homo sapiens* and no other species, which was an oversimplification, but a broader question is how far might current discussion on human evolution challenge particular religious interpretations of humanity? In other words, does the evolutionary explanation of the way things are imply that there is nothing particularly special about human beings and thereby challenge religious views, including the possibility that human capacity for wonder points to the transcendent? A sociobiologist like E. O. Wilson has to assume that our capacity for wonderment has a survival advantage, though I have my doubts about how this could ever be linked directly with reproductive prowess.

As mentioned in the last chapter, in October 2004 scientists announced the fascinating discovery of *Homo floresiensis*, a new species of human discovered on the island of Flores in Indonesia.[26] This human species, nicknamed *'hobbits'* was smaller than its ancestor, *Homo erectus*, and adapted to the particular living conditions of its island home. Our own species, *Homo sapiens*, was not unique in evolutionary history, but it did clearly out-compete its rivals, even if this happened relatively recently in the geological record. Does such a discovery undermine the meaning of humans as made in the image of God, *imago Dei*? The meaning of image-bearing needs to be able to take into account such research, but at the same time it is important to note once again that the biblical record was never intended to be a scientific document. It was, rather, a mythical narrative about human origins and their relationship to the Creator God, rather than a scientific account of how humans emerged. If we believed the latter, then women would have come from a male rib, and humans simply arrived straight from dirt, rather than through an evolutionary process. A literalist view when it comes to human origins is quite simply nonsensical. It is, therefore, a somewhat naive approach to theology to presume that such scientific discoveries undermine the validity of human image-bearing, or religious understandings of the human, or to presume that evolutionary science has the trump card in explaining what humanity is about. Henry Gee, for example, writing in the prestigious scientific journal *Nature*, argues that this discovery questions 'the security of some of our deepest beliefs'.[27] But this is only really the case if Genesis is equated with scientific accounts of evolution, which clearly it is not. It does, nonetheless, call into question any arrogance about our privileged status as humans. If we do wonder at the way life on earth has evolved, then this discovery should enhance that sense of wonderment, rather than diminish it. We could have been otherwise.

Human image-bearing has been associated in the Christian tradition with particular abilities, such as reasoning, or particular functions, such as stewardship of the earth. The former, taken to its extreme, would exclude those who have no reasoning powers, while the latter would exclude those who were not able to fulfil these functions. A more satisfactory account of image-bearing is a relational one, that is, those who bear the image are in a special relationship with God through revelation and grace. In addition, we could add that a way of expressing this special relationship with God is through wonder, as well as through wisdom. Did *Homo floresiensis* have such a relationship with God? Such a question is answerable only by God, rather than ourselves.

There will always be questions and a sense of wonderment at

the beginnings and ends of life, and for human life such beginnings and ends are also the locus of questioning and ethical discussion. The mystery and wonder of human birth remains as such, even beyond the workings of assisted reproductive technologies. It is here that discussion about the origin of life takes on particular ethical cogency. For where do we decide to trace such human origins, or more specifically, personal origins? Is it at the moment of conception or later? Certainly, where we place the line will have drastic consequences on our ethical choices. Some, in the name of ignorance, will want to take the most conservative view. Others prefer to work in the knowledge that heaven is unlikely to be populated by billions upon billions of those early human lives that have failed to implant. In any event, the origin of human life remains, as yet, outside full human control, but like the origin of life itself, even if this were known, I would argue that such beginnings are still under the Providence of God. Life's beginnings, are, in other words, something to be celebrated, a creative act that takes on particular cogency in the light of the incarnation of Christ.

CONCLUSIONS

This chapter has traced the story of wonder as experienced through life in all its diversity and complexity. Many of the early natural historians saw the wonder expressed in the diversity of life as pointing to a divine Creator. A tradition of being both a parson and naturalist was quite common; the rural parson had a sparse population to care for which allowed him to spend time observing the world about him. Darwin's theory of evolution challenged the direct link between wonder and the transcendent, in as much as views about God as Creator were tied up with notions of individual creation of species. There were some who saw evolutionary ideas as a threat to faith, but others incorporated evolution into their Christian view of the world.

As natural science dissociated itself from religious ideas a new form of wondering came to the surface, a wonder apparently shorn of its spiritual reference. Yet many scientists could see the

value of wonder even in its secularised form as a way of en-
hancing respect for life in all its richness and for the complexities
of interactions discovered by ecological science. Those biologists
who have argued for the replacement of religious ideas with
scientific wonder have failed to appreciate the religious roots of
wonderment, which cannot be explained away by reference to
Darwinian theory. Those biologists who are also believers find a
way of integrating the various aspects of wonder together, uniting
them in a transcendent vision of wonder that remains rooted in
physical and biological realities. Such a form of mysticism has
echoes of that earlier nature mystic, Francis of Assisi, but now it
is more informed by scientific knowledge. Evolutionary science
continues to knock on the door of religious beliefs, appearing to
threaten the unique status of human beings and human origins.
Yet, considered aright, new species of human beings are not so
much a threat to the wonderment about where we have come
from and where we are going to, as a means for special humility
and awe. The mystery of life remains. How far is such an
interpretation of life compatible with seeing life as part of a grand
design? Is there natural wisdom in nature, just as there is natural
wonder, and how might this relate to theological concepts of
wisdom? It is to these questions that we turn in the chapter
that follows.

THREE

NATURAL WISDOM

Is THERE WISDOM in the natural world? Certainly those natural historians highlighted in the previous chapter who celebrated the wonder of the natural world were often also conscious of a natural wisdom, in the sense of a pattern or design. In some cases they even drew moral lessons from the behaviour of animals and plants. But just as the rise of experimental science and Darwin's theory of evolution led to a reappraisal of what wonder in the natural world might mean, so too the notion of wisdom had to be re-appropriated along lines which were rather more modest about claiming that such design provided evidence for a divine designer. Yet simply viewing the natural world in mechanistic terms also seemed unsatisfying for many, allowing room for more poetic interpretations of the natural world as in some sense graced by divine action. The biblical wisdom literature also supports this notion to some extent, speaking of wisdom being found in the natural world, rather than confined to either humanity or God. More recently, evolutionary biologists have hinted that there are forms of evolutionary change that converge, that is, the process is not entirely random. I will suggest that the theological language of wisdom working within the restraints of natural law is helpful in such a context.

CREATURELY WISDOM IN SPIRITUAL PRACTICE

In the days before experimental science, the classic tradition commonly viewed the natural world as the first step on a ladder of the soul's ascent towards God. Such contemplation depended on a prior act of God's grace, purifying the soul from sinful tendencies, so that the vestiges of the wisdom of God became transparent in the natural world. For example, St Bonaventure, a Franciscan writing in 1259, claimed that:

> The supreme power, wisdom and goodness of the Creator shine forth in created things in so far as the bodily senses inform the interior senses ... In the first way of seeing, the observer considers things in themselves ... the observer can rise, as from a vestige, to the knowledge of the immense power, wisdom and goodness of the Creator. In the second way of seeing, the way of faith ... we understand that the world was fashioned by the Word of God.[1]

Bonaventure followed Augustine in attributing creaturely being with power, wisdom and goodness. He also cites the Book of Wisdom 11:21–22 in support of the idea that knowledge of creation can lead to knowledge of God. Although it is clear that Bonaventure believed that the revelation of the Word of God as revealed in Jesus Christ is 'superior' compared to the vestiges of God found in the natural world, the presence of God was a cosmic presence, since God is the Creator of all that is. For him, even before the journey towards God begins, the contemplative must:

> ... bring the natural powers of the soul under the influence of grace, which reforms them, and this he does through prayer; he must submit them to the purifying influence of justice, and this in his daily acts; he must subject them to the influence of enlightening knowledge, and this, in meditation; and finally he must hand them over to the influence of the perfecting power of wisdom, and this in contemplation. For just as no one arrives at wisdom except through grace, justice and knowledge, so it is that no one arrives at contemplation except through penetrating meditation, holy living and devout prayer.[2]

In other words, it would be a mistake to think that this form of natural theology was a way of finding God in the natural world independent of God, or that those who were habitual sinners could somehow just 'see' God in the natural order of things without prior experience of God in prayer. Bonaventure also seems to go further than this in suggesting that only those who are acting out their faith through *actions of justice,* and only those who already have some knowledge of God through *intense meditation* can begin the journey and see vestiges of the wisdom of God in the creaturely world around them. Given that the believer could reach such heights of contemplative grace, it is hardly surprising that such a view seemed antithetical to experimental science. In the early history of the church the natural world had symbolic value, pointing towards higher spiritual realities. Augustine presupposed a philosophy that followed Plato, one where the most 'real' experience was not in the visible material world at all, but rather in the eternal realm of ideas.

Yet Bonaventure did not just see the creaturely world as expressing the vestiges of God's nature, as a symbol of divine action, he also believed that faith views the world as charged with God's presence. He claimed that we need to move beyond mere vestiges, for in creatures 'He is present in them by his essence, His power and His presence.'[3] While Augustine heavily influenced him in his Platonic descriptions of creatures as 'shadows' of that perfect wisdom found in God, he also wanted to encourage careful understanding of the truth, including the truth that could come from scientific activity. Such scientific activity is put to a particular goal, namely the goal of mystical union with God. The contemplation of the insights of the various sciences takes place in charity. In other words, all knowledge and human endeavour is instilled with the spirit of love. He is able to link various aspects of human endeavour together: reading with fervour, speculation with devotion, investigation with admiration, observation with exultation, industry with piety, knowledge with love, understanding with humility, study with grace, and finally the mirror with wisdom.[4]

DOES NATURAL SCIENCE POINT TO WISDOM?

Bonaventure and others opened the way for an appreciation of a more detailed observation of the natural world that emerged eventually in the writing of John Ray and others. In addition, more mechanistic understandings of the workings of nature became much more popular in the seventeenth century. This view stated that we could understand the natural world by reference to its constituent parts. John Ray's *The Wisdom of God Manifested in the Glory of Creation* was published in 1695. Ray believed that we could arrive at a more accurate knowledge of God's wisdom through the careful study of natural history. He also went further than this, in that now the wonderful and intricate design found in the workings of the natural world could point to evidence for a designer. The world becomes a somewhat cloudy mirror of the workings of the divine Mind. For him, Nature only dimly reflected its divine origin, rather than assumed importance as a book to be read alongside Scripture. He also believed that God had designed the world for particular purposes, more often than not to serve human interests.

Some scientists who were Christians even went further than this, in suggesting that by their careful investigations they would now be able to uncover God's original purpose of creatures for human use. For example, God designed the silkworm to make silk for human benefit; God designed the camel for carrying pack-saddles, and so on. Those writing in this vein struggled to give adequate explanations of more unsavoury aspects of the natural world. Yet the design metaphor persisted, making later readers of this literature wonder at their incredulity.

In the classic tradition, observations about the natural world pointed to spiritual realities found in Scripture. In other words, the natural world was symbolic of the divine. The inverse now applied, for many natural scientists, including Isaac Newton, believed that the natural sciences led to hidden meanings of Scripture. In other words, the natural sciences helped to uncover deeper spiritual realities. While Bonaventure had argued for a general wisdom, present in all scientific research, now such general wisdom became the modicum for truth, and the means for interpretation of spiritual realities. Many scientists of the time began to question the metaphysical presumption of a two-layered reality, a world of nature and a supernatural world of spiritual beings.

The story so far suggests that even before Darwin's *Origin of Species*, the belief in a separate supernatural order had come under fire. His ideas paved the way for an explanation of creaturely purpose that removed any need for a Divinity, or correlated ideas such as a designer. The physico-theologies that had found evidence for a designer behind every instance of created existence began to look very unconvincing. Nature began to be seen as wholly autonomous, able to evolve without any particular need for divine intervention, either in the creation of new species, or in the particular workings of particular creatures. The design hypothesis also came under attack for other reasons. Not only was the natural world revealed as 'red in tooth and claw', but also some features seemed particularly puzzling. Why, for example, did certain organs, such as the appendix, persist even though they had no apparent usefulness? As evolutionary explanation accounted neatly for such anomalies the design argument fell into trouble.

How might the wisdom of God be expressed? For authors such as Henry Drummond, God could no longer be thought of in the same way; God is like a spiritual presence infusing the laws of nature. An alternative is to suggest that God simply created the process of evolution. This harks back to the classic idea of primary and secondary causes. God is the prime cause, who creates the world of secondary causes, including the processes of evolution. This view neatly avoids issues surrounding natural 'evil', for such events are outcomes of secondary causes which are detached from direct involvement with God's action. Of course, the medievalists who argued for primary and secondary causes also believed in divine Providence and the sustaining activity of God in the creativity of the world. But their view of creation was more static, so that once God had created it the world was not subject to change in the way indicated by Darwin's theory. In evolutionary theory the creative act became integral to the process itself, so that new creations emerged from secondary activities in a way that would have been anathema for the classical writers, for it would have denied the action of God in the creation of creatures. Pierre Teilhard de Chardin, who spent much of his time living in China, managed to incorporate evolutionary ideas into his theological treatise. One of his most famous books was *The Human Phenomenon*, but, as mentioned in the previous chapter, his *Divine Milieu* is also remarkable.[5] He was unusual in that he combined a mystic appreciation of the natural order with a strong commitment to Roman Catholic faith. Although the official hierarchy castigated him in his lifetime, his papers and other books were published posthumously, and he never formally left the Church. He argued for the spiritual presence of God in the whole of the cosmos, an inner psychic energy that would eventually flourish into first biogenesis, or the formation of life, then hominisation, with the appearance of consciousness, and then Christogenesis. His grand vision strikes many readers as overly optimistic, but he was writing at a time of deep pessimism, and it allowed those who wanted to affirm evolution to do so without losing their Christian faith.

Arthur Peacocke is a contemporary writer who has done much to convince others that evolution and Christian belief are compatible with each other, even suggesting that Darwin is a disguised friend for theology, as evolution serves to deepen religious understanding in the light of scientific knowledge.[6]

POETIC NATURAL WISDOM

Darwin's theory presupposed a mechanistic philosophy of nature that had been in vogue ever since Descartes' view became popular in the seventeenth century. Biologists strongly resisted vitalism, the view that there was an inner energy in life that accounted for its existence. The idea of nature as a machine conveniently dovetailed with scientific investigations, especially somewhat callous attitudes toward animal experimentation. Yet in many respects the machine metaphor seemed inadequate, and alongside such views there were others who espoused organic models for nature. According to this view, nature is viewed in more romantic terms as charged with life and energy.

The works of the seventeenth-century poet and priest Thomas Traherne is of significance, as he managed to combine a mystic, poetic and somewhat romantic view of the natural world with scientific knowledge and learning. He was simultaneously drawn to the work of the early Church Fathers, but held no fear of s-cience or scientific explanations. In this he contrasts with some of the romantic poets of the period who tended to see conventional (mechanistic) scientific activity as troublesome or even danger-ous. The romantic view of the natural world was associated with a breadth of vision along with the idea of nature as organic, holis-tic, and in some sense mysterious. Those scientists who were attracted to Romanticism appealed to the use of imagination and empathy, the trend reaching its peak in the late eighteenth cen-tury.[7] For them, conventional science 'killed' nature, but in the end the more mechanistic view prevailed, partly as a result of its practical success. But it would be incorrect to suppose that the mechanistic philosophy of Descartes dominated to such an extent that it totally annihilated the sense of the poetic among the more conventional practice of science. Instead, the beauty of the form and design revealed through natural science was an aesthetic experience.

Thomas Traherne put more emphasis on the poetic aspects of the natural world, but he still supported all scientific investiga-tions. In his earliest years he speaks of experiencing the world as spotless, pure, imbibed with the glorious presence of God, extending even to time itself, so that 'All Time was Eternity and a Perpetual Sabbath'.[8] He bewails this lost innocence, and seeks to go back to the time when he could see God in all God's works. He speaks of being aged four years old, 'prompted to, by a real Whispering Instinct of Nature. And if He be infinit in Goodness and a Perfect Being in Wisdom and Love, certainly He must do most Glorious Things: and give us infinit Riches; how comes it to pass therefore that I am so poor?'[9] In his poem, 'Thanksgivings for the Soul', he likens the world to a 'Temple of thy Wisdom, Blessedness and Glory', and it is with dread mixed with joy that he reflects on the capabilities of the human soul.[10] He also, like John Ray, marvelled at the intricate workings of nature, seeing in the creation of insects a mirror of infinite wisdom. He believed that the Wisdom of God was an active, energetic force, 'shaping painfully and at great cost, the symmetry, harmony and proportion that are the essence of all beauty'.[11] Yet the poetry that accompanies Traherne's careful observation of nature reaches new heights compared with that expressed in John Ray's writing. At heart Traherne was a spiritual writer and priest, concerned for the spiritual welfare of his readers, from whatever available relevant source. Ray, by contrast, was at heart a scientist, but he was one who was intent on using his science for the greater glory of God. Both writers were optimistic about the value of science for their religion, but while Ray enlarged upon a tradition of natural theology that was subsequently eroded by Charles Darwin, even while anticipating some of his theories, Traherne's spiritual writings, by drawing on the classical traditions, are still of some relevance, for he offers a way of appreciating the natural world as sacramental glory without giving up on science. His criticisms are directed against the political self-centredness of his time, and the powerful interweaving of politics and religion that still has some resonance today. Both authors, perhaps, were naive about the benefits of science.

NATURAL WISDOM IN THE HEBREW BIBLE

John Ray and Thomas Traherne were drawn to the wisdom literature. They lacked sophistication in biblical exegesis. The question we might ask now is, are there any biblical precedents for finding wisdom in the natural world? At the outset we need to remind ourselves that the biblical writers were ignorant of what we now call natural sciences. I suggest that given the incorrect tendency to read science into Scripture, most notably in stories about the beginning and the creation of the world, we need to avoid finding particular scientific insights in the biblical text. However, we can, legitimately, ask a different question, namely were there, according to the views of the Hebrew sages, any benefits in paying particular attention to the natural world? As a people they would have been far more vulnerable to the forces of the natural world compared with current experience, though every now and then a dramatic earthquake or volcanic eruption reminds us that we cannot predict with absolute accuracy all that happens in the world around us.

The Book of Proverbs, Chapter 8, describes wisdom as the first of God's creatures, ever at play in creation, at play with God in the creation of the world. Yet it is clear that wisdom is not the same as creation, but is to some extent distinct from it, but alongside God in all creative acts. Proverbs 6:6 is rather more explicit about the possibility of learning something about wisdom from observing the natural world in the injunction to the sluggard to 'go to the ant … see its ways and be wise'. But what does seeing mean? Careful exegesis of this term suggests that seeing here is not so much detailed observation of the workings of ant behaviour, however complex that might be, but perceiving the distinctive inner core or 'way' of what it is to be an ant.[12] In other places in the wisdom literature we find the word discernment after the act of seeing; this word describes the process of becoming wise. Discernment in this case is not just about a correct choice where there are a number of different options, but accurately identifying the inner driving characteristic of something. It is, if you like, a way of showing empathy with the creatures under view, a 'feeling for the organism' in the manner of Barbara McClintock. A similar sentiment is in Proverbs 30:18–19, which is also interesting as it links the search for wisdom with wonder:

> Three things are too wonderful for me;
> Four I do not understand:
> The way of an eagle in the sky,
> The way of a snake on a rock,
> The way of a ship on the high seas,
> The way of a man with a young woman.

Does this way of seeing rule out careful observation of different characteristics? In other words, does it rule out scientific research? I suggest that it does not, but it does imply respect for whatever is under investigation.

The Book of Job is particularly interesting as it describes God as finding wisdom, 'seeing' and, by implication, appreciating, the different components of creation. On this basis we could take the next step and suggest that Proverbs 8 speaks about God as *acquiring* wisdom, rather than *creating* wisdom, which is the more common translation.[13] If God acquires wisdom through seeing the works of creation, then this might imply a deep natural wisdom which in some sense then echoes back into the divine Wisdom. If we follow this route, does it still make sense to speak about God creating through Wisdom? I suggest that it does, for the movement of creating is always in love, so that there is a waiting on the part of God for a creaturely response. Such a response, such natural wisdom, reaches particular poignancy in human image-bearing, but this does not rule out the possibility of wisdom also finding echoes in other aspects of creation.

In the Book of Job, Chapter 12, Job accuses God of misusing his power, destroying innocent earthly creatures along with errant humans. The reply God makes simply reminds him that the cosmos is ordered, rather than chaotic, but God does not answer the charges made. The ordering that the Book of Job describes is that according to the inner characteristic of all beings, or its inner wisdom. Each aspect of creation expresses this inner wisdom in a distinctive way. The Book of Job is a clear reminder that the whole of creation is to be celebrated because of this diversity of wisdom; in other words, creatures are not simply there to serve human ends. In addition, there is no sense in trying to tame wild animals or domesticate them for human ends – the wild ox has to be left in its wild state. The Hebrew scholar Norman Habel suggests that 'All the phenomena of Earth, it seems, have wisdom within them; wisdom is not only something humans acquire by observing nature. It also seems to be something embedded in nature that humans are challenged to discover.'[14]

Alongside this tradition, which recognises that creatures know how best to behave through an inner sense, we find acknowledgement that ultimately all creatures are dependent on God. Hence divine Providence remains intact, even if humanity discovers why it is that creatures behave in the way that they do. Job 39:1–4 also pays particular attention to the way creatures give birth at the appropriate times, an unfolding dynamic that points to more than just a fixed ordering of the cosmos. The ostrich was one bird that, for the writers following the folklore of the period, appeared to abandon its young. Why? According to the author the reason is simple: the ostrich lacked inner wisdom. What is the response of Job to these inklings of natural wisdom in all its diversity? He is filled with wonder and praise for the Creator of all.

NATURAL WISDOM IN EVOLUTIONARY BIOLOGY

How far have scientists begun to probe the inner wisdom characteristic of the natural world spoken about in poetic terms in the Book of Job? While we looked at the cosmic origin and the timeline of the first life on the planet in Chapter 1, there are other questions that we can probe about life in relation to why it is the way it is, and what makes for common ground and diversity among species. Scientists know now the molecular basis for life in a way that was largely opaque in previous centuries. Twenty different amino acids are available to make up chains of a hundred or so in order to form proteins. The potential number of different proteins is 100^{20}, that is 10^{39}.[15] If we presume that one in a million proteins is water soluble, and one in a million has the right sort of shape for it to be active as an enzyme, which is the function of most proteins, then the number of possible proteins still exceeds the number of stars in the universe. Why is the actual number of proteins on earth so much smaller than this? One reason is that it is not really necessary for evolution to try out all the different combinations of amino acids along the whole chain of the protein; it is only the active site which defines protein function that is really important, as well as some other areas that specify the way the protein folds up. The architectural forms are very important for some proteins, resulting in the transparency of eye lenses, the ability to store oxygen and the sensitivity to light in light-sensitive proteins such as rhodopsin and cryptochromes. In other words, particular protein architecture specifies function, and this may involve very different combinations of amino acids and evolutionary pathways. There is *convergence* at the molecular level of proteins, different evolutionary pathways leading to similarly shaped proteins. Similar analysis of the genetic code shows that if we randomise a million different codes, then most codes are reasonably efficient. However, what is surprising is that the actual genetic code found in the natural world is some two orders of magnitude more efficient than those codes produced by random combinations. Why might this be the case? The genetic code is common to all life forms and conserved in a remarkable way. The fact that it also happens to be virtually the best of all possible codes out of the 270 million different possible alternatives remains a puzzle for biologists to explain, unless the real possibilities were actually very much fewer than this. The palaeontologist Simon Conway Morris suggests that 'life shows a kind of homing instinct', so that 'despite its fecundity and baroque richness life is also strongly restrained'.[16]

Yet the phenomenon of convergence is not just confined to the molecular hyperspace – evolutionary biologists have found similar functions and architectural form at the level of organs and species as well.[17] If adaptation by natural selection is the most important, then this is what one would expect, that is, convergence of many different species and genetic lineages to given environments. In other words, if we re-ran the tape of life again, it would in all probability be reasonably similar, at least in form and function, to life as we see it today. Even human intelligence or something like it would have appeared as a matter of course over enough time. Of course, more traditionally, evolutionary biologists have put much more emphasis on the contingent aspects of the course of evolution. If chance plays a key role in diversity, then populations would be expected to evolve in all kinds of diverse ways. According to this view, if we re-ran the tape of life again, we would have very different forms of life appearing, and in all probability we would not find any intelligent beings. However, I think that the smart money is on the more radical idea of evolutionary constraint. I will describe a few more examples to illustrate the point. Convergence does not need to imply some kind of 'end point', though repeat convergence does imply a kind of 'stability' of given biological habitable zones. In addition, evolution is still open to change even after reaching a level of fitness to a given set of conditions. Wonder accompanies much of the discoveries of convergence; some palaeontologists have even called the phenomenon 'eerie' or 'uncanny'.

Both the marsupial thylacosmilid and the placental cat, for example, have similarly enormous sabre teeth, though the specific structures of the teeth are slightly different. Again, we can find an eel-like morphology of fish from the North American brook lamprey, neotropical swamp eels and African spiny eel. Other characteristic pike-like morphology appears in very different lineages. Similar morphological convergence appears among desert plants, for example cacti and spurges. Among birds we find convergences in a range of characteristics among migrants, or among grain- and insect-eating birds, or aquatic birds, or in the case of the hummingbirds' convergence with the sphinx moth, both hovering above flowers in order to feed on the nectar. Similar chemical defences to attack in the form of steroidal alkaloids are also common to a New Guinea bird known as *Pitohui* and a Neotropical poison dart frog. Among burrowing mammals there are evolutionary convergences in anatomy, physiology, behaviour and in some cases genetics across three orders, 11 families and 150 genera. Examples of some typical characteristics are small eyes, strong forelimbs with powerful claws, and small testicles.

As is well known, many insect groups have eusociality, which is the establishment of a colony with one reproductive female and remaining castes of workers, as in bees, wasps, ants, termites and some beetles. Remarkably enough, eusociality has also evolved among mammals several times, for example in particular groups of mole rats and voles, as well as in the crustacean, the coral reef shrimp. The particular evolutionary trajectory is different for each species that shows convergence, but the final destinations seem to be more limited than one might expect. Examples of convergence are legion, but it is worth mentioning the camera eye, as this has evolved independently in cephalopods, such as the squid and the octopus, in vertebrates, such as humans, and in annelids, which are marine relatives of the common earthworm. Yet camera eyes are also found in cubozoan jellyfish, and even though these simple creatures do not have a brain, they do show sophisticated behaviour. Finally, biologists have discovered a kind of camera eye in a hunting spider called the *Dinopis*, though almost all arthropods have compound eyes that are very different in structure. If humans were to rely on compound eyes they would need to be about a metre across; camera eyes are much more efficient. Yet for camera and compound eyes, and simpler forms such as eyespots, the crystalline proteins of the eye lens give translucence to the lens. Historically these proteins evolved in order to give resistance to physiological stress, especially heat shock. It shows how complex structures could gradually build up over the course of evolution, and materials at one time useful for one function are then co-opted or redeployed for different functions. Natural evolutionary wisdom makes use of what is readily available, rather than trying to invent something from scratch. More examples of convergences, in the capacity of different species for smell, hearing, sentience, intelligence and so on, could fill up this entire book. Also, as I mentioned earlier, given that humanity has only identified a fraction of existing species and only described a small fraction of these in any detail, ignorance must be the byword when it comes to understanding the full richness of biodiversity currently on the planet, quite apart from the myriad forms yet to be identified in the fossil record.

Are we now better informed about the 'way' of the ant? Certainly, natural wisdom might indicate that convergence implies some similarity of form, function and behaviour across different species. The ways show some parallels. Why call this natural wisdom and not design? Design implies a deliberate designer, and although this metaphor might have had some usefulness in the past, it has fallen foul of critics who can point to a legion of inconsistencies in this approach. It also implies force acting from the 'outside', as it were, crafting individual species in order to serve particular functions. Natural wisdom, by contrast, puts more emphasis on the process of the evolutionary searchlight, specifically scanning those forms of biological diversity that are available in what Simon Conway Morris has termed 'habitable biospace', improvising on what has been used in the past, rather than creating complex forms from scratch. Yet full convergence across all traits simultaneously has not yet been found, for the way/wisdom of each species is unique. As G. K. Chesterton once remarked 'there is probably a beetle view of things of which a man is entirely ignorant.'[18]

IS EVOLUTION PURPOSEFUL?

For a biologist, the idea of purposefulness in terms of intended and deliberate outcome flies in the face of evolutionary processes of chance and necessity. In other words, the evolution of biodiversity in life is about the chance variation of natural mutations working within the constraints of physical laws. Yet it is highly unlikely that the complex processes of convergence are a simple outcome of the restraint of physical laws. Rather, novel kinds of constraints seem to be working in many cases, even though biologists are not able to identify the precise reasons for such convergent constraints. This is one reason for the sense of awe, or eerie feeling, that evolutionary biologists feel, for it touches the edge of a mystery. Does such a sense of mystery imply a spirituality or divine origin? I would be wary of locating God purely in this area of unknowing, even though it is tempting for cosmologists to do so in speaking about the origin of the habitable earth in which life became possible. But profound feelings of awe are compatible with a religious sense, so that where a religious instinct is present, then this can deepen still further religious belief.

I will be coming back to the sense of a journey into wonder in a later chapter, but for now I want to confine the discussion to thinking more specifically about evolution and purpose. Would feelings of awe disappear if a 'natural' explanation could be found in order to explain more fully the phenomenon of convergence? I suggest it would not; rather it would simply deepen our understanding of natural wisdom. Perhaps the idea of evolutionary purpose is a misnomer when it comes to speaking about convergence, for it is making a more modest claim, namely that evolution is not entirely free to explore every possible variation that could be conceived of as existing. Is restriction the same as purpose? I doubt it, but it differs from randomness as well.

What theological parallel might help in this respect? My suggestion is that convergence has some parallels with the theological idea of natural law. Although, like other theological categories, natural law is unashamed of a sense of purpose, in that its goal is that good is sought and evil avoided, but it has other characteristics as well. Natural law is a description of the constrictions in behaviour that humankind finds as inherent in biological capabilities.[19] Natural law posits that there are stable forms of behaviour which seem to be common, regardless of the particular societies in which humanity is based. The classic tradition believed that natural law was capable of being adopted by diverse human societies, though recognised that there would be local variations, just as we might find local variations in the way convergence is expressed, depending on historical origin. As such it is a very broad theological category that recognises the importance of human biological origins. Yet, it announces a significant departure from convergence in that it also points towards a self-confessed sense of purpose.

What is the origin of this feeling of purpose that is intrinsic to natural law? Certainly, for Aquinas, natural law is participation by rational creatures in the 'Eternal Law'. The Eternal Law is expressive of God's being, so that, through participation, rational creatures find a way of discovering the underlying purposefulness and meaning that is inherent in their existence. Aquinas also realised that all creaturely being had some share in the Eternal Law, but it only becomes self-conscious in rational creatures. Does this mean that now we need to widen the net of rational creatures to include not just humans, but also other highly intelligent species such as some species of birds or social mammals? This remains, I think, an open question; the point is not so much which creatures are consciously participating in the Eternal Law, but rather, a sense of the unity of all creaturely being. For biologists the notion of purpose is a convenient illusion, helping different species to search out those options that are best suited for survival and reproduction. Unfortunately, the outcome of adopting the idea of evolution as a metaphysics means that we are left with meaninglessness: ultimately life is pointless. Theologians disagree in this respect, in that purposefulness or meaningfulness is inherent to their understanding of God as Creator, regardless of how far they believe that purposefulness might be expressed. Hence, if we try to force Darwin's theory of evolution into a metaphysical explanation of reality, we are left with frustration and disappointment. Instead, it needs to be celebrated as a way of helping us understand natural wisdom. Convergence is a language about evolution that opens up the window once more for biologists to explore the concept of purpose, just as natural law opens up a window once more for theologians to affirm biological insights as having significance. The two areas of discussion are deliberately held up as to some extent analogous with the other, opening up a deeper appreciation of the richness of the biological world in all its dimensions.

What more might we say about this analogy from a theological perspective? The Eternal Law is also closely connected with the Wisdom of God, and just as natural law could be thought of as a participation in the Eternal Law, so natural wisdom could be thought of as a form of participation in divine Wisdom. Participation implies difference, and yet intimacy, both of which are important when considering analogies more generally between God and the natural world. This analogy between being and 'Being' is one of the reasons why we find the beautiful in the natural world, and one of the reasons why we are led to a sense of awe in contemplation of natural wisdom. For natural wisdom takes us to the foothills of divine Wisdom, but it can never be confused with it, for such confusion amounts to idolatrous illusion. Strong neo-Darwinians, such as Richard Dawkins, are famous for speaking of religious believers as those suffering from illusions. It is well known that Charles Darwin himself went through a period when he seemed to hold onto a pantheistic view of the world, confusing the world with God, prior to giving up his belief altogether. Yet the residual shadow of wonder continued to haunt him, like the afterglow of the Big Bang. From a theological perspective, illusionary images of the Divine amount to a confusion of the creation with the Creator, of failing to see the difference, more often than not leading to an outcome of despair or resignation.

CONCLUSIONS

I began this chapter with an exploration of the classic texts of St Bonaventure who, in the thirteenth century, spoke of natural wisdom as a vestige of the wisdom of God existing in the created world. He believed that those of faith could see such a vestige as the first step on the ladder of ascent towards God, culminating in deep mystical experience. The seventeenth century gave birth to experimental science, and authors like John Ray believed that meticulous scientific observation of nature led scientists to the Wisdom of God, but it was a faded mirror of perfection.

The idea that the design in the natural world pointed to an author of that design or divine designer soon found itself in trouble once Charles Darwin had formulated a naturalistic explanation of the origin of species. Some theologians became adept at incorporating their theological belief with evolutionary theory.

The twentieth-century Jesuit priest and palaeontologist Pierre Teilhard de Chardin was one of the most influential writers in this vein. Teilhard could also be thought of as a poet, as well as a scientist, and in this he echoes the work of seventeenth-century writers such as Thomas Traherne, who tried to combine a deep appreciation of natural science with a poetic sensitivity to the world around him. How far does the wisdom literature support the notion of natural wisdom? Hebrew scholars are more inclined to think of wisdom as discernment once we pay due attention to the inner workings of a particular creature, for example the way of an ant. Even God, it seems, celebrates this diversity in all creatures, and thereby gains in wisdom. Perhaps this is a way of expressing more fully the interpenetration of God's Wisdom with creaturely wisdom, that there is a sense in which this creativity continues to unfold.

What might evolutionary debates suggest about natural wisdom? Evolutionary biologists often couch the passage of evolution in terms of a random, almost meaningless walk through time. Yet another story is now emerging, one that speaks of restriction, rather than randomness, one that highlights convergence in numerous different traits in some unexpected ways. How are we to fathom such convergence? Current biological explanations seem too limited. Yet within a theological framework such convergence can make sense, for theology is not ashamed to admit to purposefulness in the unfolding of creation and its sustained activity. God is not so much filling in the gaps of knowledge; rather, given a theistic view, the passage of convergence takes on a richer meaning. Biologists must still, needless to say, carry on in their search for natural explanations. Theologians, on the other hand, relate natural wisdom to divine Wisdom, just as natural law is related to the Eternal Law. But is there something special about human wisdom, or is it just a form of natural wisdom? What does it mean to say that humans have wisdom, and how might we go about searching for it? It is to these questions that we turn in the chapter that follows.

FOUR

HUMAN WISDOM

I HAVE SUGGESTED so far that all creatures, including humans, share in natural wisdom. What are the specific characteristics of human wisdom and does it make sense to distinguish this from natural wisdom? Is wisdom an evolved capacity, aligned with intelligence? What is the psychology of human wisdom and how might this relate to a theological approach to wisdom? More important, perhaps, is a theology of human wisdom defensible in the light of current psychological and neurological explanations of human cognition? I will argue the case that theology brings to bear dimensions on human wisdom that go beyond scientific explanations, even if it is true that science illuminates aspects of that wisdom. Also, the classical notion of wisdom as prudence is helpful in outlining what human wisdom means in terms of ethical practice.

ARE HUMANS SPECIAL?

I suggested in the last chapter that a key characteristic of natural wisdom is the inner capacity for something to be itself, the way or inner driving characteristic of a creature, and by extension, what makes humans the way they are, developed in a particular way through human consciousness. Highly developed consciousness is a precondition of the ability to wonder and also human wisdom. Human consciousness brings with it a sense of being a unique self, or subjectivity and, in as much as this is the case, it eludes description by neurological science. While still in some sense elusive, scientists continue to probe this area, opening up important insights as to how this might be related to brain function.[1] Part of the problem for science has to do with the definition of consciousness, for human imagination stretches far into the universe. Yet most definitions try to capture aspects of what it is to feel like to be an 'I', a sense of time that encompasses past, present and future concerns, a sense that we act out of deliberate decisions rather than as automata. *Consciousness* is related to what we feel when we are awake, whereas our *minds* bring with them the connotation of a more enduring state of mental health that is integral to our personalities. Consciousness also grows with development and deepens as the brain becomes more sophisticated from foetus to neonate to child. Yet neuroscience suggests that even our minds are a kind of 'ecosphere' of ideas, harbouring tunes and phrases that then gradually reshape the neuronal connections in our brains. Scientists cannot say how the neuronal connections in our brains 'cause' a sense of consciousness, but experiments can rule out certain presumptions. For example, consciousness seems to be a distributed function throughout the brain, rather than isolated to a single area or brain region. Different bundles of neurones seem to work together for a period of time, and then others take over.

Does consciousness exist in other life forms? If scientists give the simple sea slug, *Aplysia*, an electric shock, it reacts by retracting its gill. It does not react to a gentle touch, but if it receives the touch and electric shock together, then later on it reacts to the gentle touch. This simple 'memory' is the outcome of a linear relay of neuronal impulses, a one-to-one correspondence between neuronal memory and behaviour. The mammalian memory is very much more sophisticated, in that while it also requires neuronal impulses, there is much more complexity involved. In other words, there are emergent properties that depend on a whole host of other issues as well. Simpler organisms do not seem to need sleep, but the rest period is not so dramatically different from the active, moving state in terms of electrical activity of the neuronal cells. It seems very likely that such creatures have a low sense of consciousness.

Any sharp distinction between humans and other animals in the manner that Descartes supposed is ill founded; rather, there are grades of conscious activity. Mammals, in particular, have a capacity for memory that makes them candidates for a more highly developed state of consciousness. More advanced levels of consciousness allow for what some biologists have called a 'higher order' consciousness, a self-awareness bringing with it the ability to daydream, reminisce and speculate. Is such self-awareness unique to humans? Experiments suggest that even rats have some sort of capacity for forming internal representations as distinct from the immediate physical appearance of an object. Hence, a distinction between levels of consciousness is not particularly useful; there is, rather, a continuum of change from the simplest creatures to the more advanced mammalian species. Such a continuum also suggests that using human consciousness as a way of arguing for the existence of God does not take us very far. Consciousness is an emergent property in evolved living creatures, even if human consciousness is very much more sophisticated.

The view that there is a continuum between humans and other creatures also extends to other related areas such as intelligence. Evolutionary biologists divide over the issue of how far brain development and associated intelligence arose as a result of contingent events, or whether it was an inevitable process as a result of inbuilt constraints, converging on certain forms. Stephen Jay Gould opted for the random approach, suggesting that if evolution happened again, then we would not be here now. Simon Conway Morris disagrees, arguing that evolution is bounded by constraints, so humans are not so much chance products of evolution, but the evolution of something like us is more or less inevitable.[2] Such constraints imply that the course of evolution is not as random as one might think, but it has a direction to it, homing in on some avenues rather than others, akin to a compass needle helping the mariner in uncharted seas.

Most mammals have a brain that matches their body mass, but some have disproportionately larger brains. Elephants, chimpanzees and dolphins all have progressively bigger brains relative to their body mass. Humans have brains seven times bigger relative to their body mass. High intelligence might seem like an evolutionary accident, not serving any particular evolutionary advantage. Yet this view seems pretty unlikely, for those primates with larger brains have more sophisticated behaviour, social learning and tool use. But can we take the next step and suggest that the evolution of intelligence is inevitable? If we compare the relative brain size of dolphins with our nearest evolutionary neighbours, *Homo erectus* and *Homo habilis*, then their relative brain sizes are all comparable. Why did the brain size increase relative to body mass in dolphins? The change took place at a time when the southern oceans cooled dramatically, providing a significant environmental challenge. Larger brain size in *Homo* species also seemed to be associated with more challenging environmental conditions, in their case a very arid environment in the African subcontinent.

Yet larger brain sizes persisted over time, most probably associated with the emergence of complex social organisation. Biologists have found that sperm whales and elephants exhibit somewhat remarkable parallels in behaviour, which shows commonalities that exceed those relating to their nearest evolutionary neighbours. In the social groups of both species, the females form close-knit groups with their young, while males are more solitary. The bottle-nosed dolphins also show remarkable parallels with chimpanzees in terms of their social complexity and organisation, even though they diverged many millennia before in evolutionary terms and occupy very different ecological niches. Individuals in both groups show the capacity for movement in and out of social groups, and research also suggests that dolphins can form 'super-alliances' of at least 100 individuals.

Dolphins make sounds, 'vocalisations' that are far more sophisticated than we might suppose. Similar trends exist in birds, many corvids (such as crows) displaying highly intelligent behaviour and vocalisations, hence challenging the notion that language is a unique capacity among humans. Fascinatingly, young dolphins go through similar stages to humans in learning their language, including babbling, eventually developing a 'signature whistle'. Biologists have also taught dolphins an artificial language based on the sounds of their whistles. This research shows that dolphins are capable of recognising both word order and meaning, with a capacity for accelerated learning over and above routine training methods. Such trends provide evidence for convergence in the way language develops.

Dolphins also show a remarkable capacity for memory, developing short-term memory, as in humans, by internal representations. What about sleep? In order to prevent drowning by not coming to the surface, one half of the dolphin brain is asleep while the other half is active. Birds also adopt a similar way of combining the need for sleep, associated with higher levels of consciousness, with the need to stay alert. It is important not to 'read into' dolphin behaviour, or primate behaviour, equivalent behaviour in humans. Brains of both primates and dolphins have enlarged cerebella, but there are important differences in the folding and development of some areas. In other words, distinctions remain but similarities indicate constraints within which evolution works. Simon Conway Morris speculates 'Human language may, on this planet, be unique, but waiting in the wings of the theatre of consciousness are other minds stirring, poised on the threshold of articulation.'[3]

Highly intelligent birds, such as corvids, and chimpanzees also show the development of tool use. This kind of research provides evidence for sophisticated intelligence over and above cruder indications given by brain size. Entomologists have also found fairly complex tool use among wasps and other insects. Such behaviour shows a multiplicity of intelligence among different species, but underlying capacities for certain actions arrive through very different intelligences and evolutionary routes. It also supports the idea that complex behaviours are convergent, rather than having arisen by accident. Also, the human ability to walk upright, or bipedality, has evolved more than once in the course of evolution. Among the apes, an extinct bipedal species named *Oreopithecus* flourished about 7 million years ago.

Careful study of the evolution of *Homo* species shows that *Homo sapiens* is the sole survivor of multiple branches of *Homo* species, supported still further by the recent discovery of the new species of small humans, *Homo floresiensis*. Research also indicates that increase in brain size occurred more than once in the course of hominid evolution, hence it is not unique to *H. sapiens*. The increase in brain size also seems to be associated with tool use; those with larger brains would have a more developed capacity and so be at a selective advantage. There was some increase in sophistication with the controlled use of fire from about 400,000 years ago. The earliest tools of the Mousterian culture were relatively unsophisticated. A more dramatic expansion in abilities appeared about 50,000 years ago in the Upper Palaeolithic period in what is known as the development of the Aurignacian culture. There were some hints in this direction about 70,000 years ago. *H. sapiens* in the Aurignacian culture had sophisticated tool kits, ornaments, and perhaps musical instruments, even though anatomically equivalent *H. sapiens* appeared earlier than this, about 125,000 years ago. *Homo neanderthalensis* is more likely to be a separate species from *H. sapiens*. Research suggests that this species, too, was capable of looking after its infirm members, and had some form of culture, as indicated by the use of fire, body paint, and possibly burial rites. *H. neanderthalensis* clearly used tools, almost certainly used language, and had tools similar to those of *H. sapiens* in the Mousterian cultural phase. Did they move beyond this stage in the manner of *H. sapiens*? Although this species did develop more advanced capabilities much later than humans, there is evidence that about 35,000 years ago they were capable of making more advanced tools and other artefacts, including jewellery. While until recently many scholars thought that their abilities came from imitating the more sophisticated Aurignacian culture of *H. sapiens*, another more controversial alternative is that these abilities were convergent, that is, they acquired such characteristics independently.

EVOLUTIONARY PSYCHOLOGY AND WISDOM

The above account shows that the boundaries between humans and other creatures, at least in terms of complex behaviour, are blurred, even though the evolutionary lineage may be very different. Is there any evidence for an evolutionary origin for more complex behavioural traits? Evolutionary psychology asserts that it is worth asking this question, and more fundamentalist approaches try to explain behaviour in terms of adaptive advantages.[4] Historically, the debate raged between those who followed Darwin and argued that even complex behaviours in humans are augmentations of those found in other primate species, and others, more in the tradition of his contemporary, Alfred Russel Wallace (1823–1913), who argued that humans possessed a God-given intelligence that exceeded what was required for simple survival. The stark alternative that specifically human characteristics are either given by God or by nature is not all that sensible. Darwin was mistaken in viewing complex human behaviours as simple augmentations of those found in primates, as similar behaviours can arise from different evolutionary pathways. Wallace was mistaken in his assumption that theism entailed God intervening in the world from the outside, regardless of natural endowment. Both ignored the role of culture in helping to shape complex behaviour, leading to contemporary debates about whether culture and genetics are two separate modes of inheritance.[5]

Research on the evolution of altruism and the ability to co-operate is a good example of how evolutionary studies in non-human species have influenced evolutionary psychology. Darwin underestimated the degree to which both animal and human species display altruistic behaviour. His theory of natural selection presupposed a nature 'red in tooth and claw'. Evolutionary biologists have tried to explain co-operative behaviour by reference to the core concepts of kinship and reciprocal altruism. Animals that help their genetic relatives do so, according to the kinship theory, because they are genetically related to them. This includes helping direct offspring, but also helping siblings or nieces or nephews in proportion to the closeness to one's kin. But how might one explain giving help to those unrelated in genetic terms? Here the theory of 'tit for tat' tries to explain how help might be offered according to the likelihood of receiving help back, a 'cost/benefit' analysis which soon picks up on those who 'cheat'. How illuminating is this for understanding human behaviour? Such models may take us a certain distance, but even a cursory overview of human history would show examples of altruism that are not so much based on self-interest, or any possibility of a reward, but seem to be genuinely self-sacrificial. Of course, an evolutionary biologist might claim that such self-sacrificial behaviour would promote esteem, which would then elevate the status of the individual in a community, bringing advantages. However, such reasoning sounds somewhat convoluted, and ignores the notable cultural shift that took place in human Aurignacian culture. The most we might say is that where examples of altruism appear in non-human species, then this implies a convergence in that trait, rather than a direct evolutionary linkage. Also, while there are some examples of human behaviour that are consistent with this view, the level and complexity of altruism cannot simply be explained by reference to evolutionary advantage.

The evolution of *Homo sapiens* does show far greater sophistication than that of animals, so too close an analogy may hinder rather than clarify human evolutionary history. Certainly, we could suppose that large brains evolved and conferred some advantage in evolutionary terms allowing more sophisticated communication in larger social groups. Also, it would be a mistake to see human behavioural traits as simply 'more advanced' stages beyond those found in animals, as the evolutionary histories are likely to be very much more convoluted than this. The most complex cultural behaviour seems to depend on a relatively large brain/mass index, even though such behaviour was strictly speaking superfluous to survival requirements. Evolutionary psychologists have speculated that the more sophisticated Aurignacian culture came indirectly from changes in social life that perhaps eventually promoted a change in 'wiring' of the neuronal networks of the brain. According to this view the last major change in evolutionary capability of humans took place in this period, so that behaviours that had survival advantage in the Aurignacian period are still in place.

What about the evolution of human wisdom? Evolutionary psychology identifies wisdom in the first place as a way of thinking, a cognitive process that leads to a particular way of obtaining or processing information. Evolutionary biologists presume such processes have survival value, either directly or indirectly through other accompanying traits. Human wisdom, according to the view of evolutionary psychology, would have adaptive value for the species.[6] One approach assumes that ideas that have survival value are 'memes', which are selected and transmitted across generations, regardless of whether the originators have biologically related offspring or not. The difficulty with meme theory is that it proposes a dualistic form of inheritance, memes seemingly being detached from genetic trends. The difficulty with an alternative strong evolutionary theory, which claims that all traits are grounded in genetics, is that it does not account adequately for many examples of complex human behaviour, including, for example, celibacy and, arguably, complex traits such as wisdom. Neither option debated among evolutionary biologists seems very satisfactory, which explains why theologians, social scientists and others have argued that science alone cannot give an adequate account. More mediating approaches that try to find common ground between religious views and biological explanations still have to face the uncomfortable truth that the underlying anthropology for most evolutionary psychologists is one of self-interest, while religious approaches stress moving away from strictly egotistic approaches.[7] Curiously, perhaps, if we apply the dual inheritance concept of genes and memes strictly to science, then even ideas arising out of science may eventually prove less helpful and so be discarded.

Wisdom as a cognitive process deals with what are perceived to be overarching universal truths, though both ancient and modern scholars disagree about what this might mean. Plato, for example, believed that the 'real' world was that of ideas, whereas the material world was simply that of appearances. More important, perhaps, wisdom as cognition implies a way of integrating different interpretations, rather than simply accumulating more information. More contemporary psychological studies indicate that a wise person has a general competence in both intelligence and technical ability, pragmatic knowledge based on experience, as well as reflective and evaluative skills. Wisdom in psychological terms has some parallels with what is known as optimal adult psychological development, which includes the ability to assume contrary viewpoints, recognition of inter-relatedness and an integrative approach to thinking. Both ancient and contemporary approaches propose that wisdom involves recognition of the importance of self-examination and a standing back in order to try and recognise the whole.

Classical psychology in Aristotle also names wisdom as a virtue, or a socially valued habitual pattern of behaviour. Wisdom is a public virtue as it takes into account the long-term consequences for the system as a whole. Modern psychology has shown how much early childhood influences can distort behaviour in later life. It is also more aware that other people's opinions might influence human judgement. In addition, the symbolic world in which we live can influence the way in which we think and make decisions. Is wisdom as a virtue still possible in the light of these insights? I would argue that such psychological studies could illuminate barriers to the attainment of wisdom as virtue, rather than disprove either its possibility or its benefits.

According to the classical tradition, wisdom also gives rise to personal goods, including joy. Wisdom also teaches through indirect means, facilitating enjoyment of discovery in the one who learns. An evolutionary psychologist would dismiss those good emotions arising out of a sense of metaphysical perception as illusory, as they would discount metaphysics. Yet if wisdom leads to a sense of well-being, an optimal state of enjoyment in consciousness, then it can have transformational power in the manner of Abraham Maslow's notion of personal 'peak' experiences. A secularised psychology affirms such heightened awareness, but detaches it from its theological roots that point not simply to individual self-satisfaction, but to a good beyond self in theism. Secular psychology recognises that there are implicit dangers in wisdom in as much as it can lead to a sense of superiority, or disorientating grandiosity, isolating self from others. But it has little to say on how to avoid such dangers.

PHILOSOPHY AND WISDOM

As hinted above, the classical writers developed their own particular views about what human wisdom might be; philosophy itself
means love of wisdom. Socrates believed that the search for wisdom was the way to live one's life. Philosophy challenges any
hints in the above account that might indicate human beings are
somehow 'programmed' to behave in certain ways. Such accounts
have a certain appeal as they can lead to a reassurance as to why
someone has acted in the way they have. Genetic determinism
presupposes that human behaviour is an outcome of our particular genetic make up; psychological determinism that humans
behave because of, for example, early experiences as an infant;
sociological determinism that humans are simply conditioned by
society; and divine determinism that God pre-ordains in advance
of individual decision.[8] Peter Vardy suggests that awareness of
human freedom as opposed to being programmed by any number
of determinisms leads to anxiety, anguish and despair. But this is
also a sign of hope, as from this position people can come to
behave in a way that goes against over-inflated egotistic desires or
convention provided by ethical rules in conformity to the group.
He believes that many people today do not live according to their
full potential; they are trapped in unreflective habits of mind. He
suggests that we need instead to recover integrated ways of thinking.

What might that integrated thinking include? In the first place
it challenges the idea that human identity is simply received in a
passive way as a given, either through genetic endowment or
'memetic' passing on of culture. This is because the way humans
live together, the symbolic realm that humans inhabit and the
networks of information that humans construct are as much
working projects as given facts.[9] In this sense, I suggest that it is
incorrect to see wisdom simply in terms of the 'transmission' of
cultural 'memes', for wisdom that is simply accepted as a given
'fact' amounts to imitation, rather than internal appropriation

and development. Of course, our biological and psychological endowment make it more likely that some individuals will have a more developed sense of wisdom than others, but we cannot explain wisdom just by reference to such capabilities. Aristotle argued that every living creature had a soul, or principle of organisation. Such a principle eventually leads to the creature becoming what it is intended to be. Wisdom is like a search of the soul, so such a search is not 'detached' from our biological make up, even if wisdom as a complex cultural capacity goes beyond biological programming.

Human wisdom is also about relational knowing that seeks to incorporate scientific knowing as one dimension in an overall picture of the whole. Nicholas Lash believes that scientific thinking about human knowledge has followed in the tradition of the seventeenth-century scientist Francis Bacon, who argued that history flows from memory, poetry from imagination, and science/philosophy from reason.[10] Such a scheme dissociates memory from argument and experience from reason, and imagination becomes relegated to the poetic way of thinking. He suggests that this reduces the significance of storytelling, of parable and of paradoxical ways of thinking. The scientific project becomes a way of homogenising other forms of knowledge; history becomes simply a receiving of facts that are passed on to the next generation. Commenting on Bacon's psychology he suggests that 'There is no sense of his being part of a story, or set of stories, which have shaped his world and made things the way they are or seem to be; no sense of his being caught up in conversation, part of some larger set of narratives that he must enact, interpret, endorse or struggle to revise.'[11] Of course, some scientists are perhaps now more aware than Bacon seemed to be of the importance of imagination, and in particular the ability to wonder. Yet those committed to evolutionary psychology tend to stray in the Baconian direction; memetic or other versions of evolutionary psychology become the means through which scientists try to capture all kinds of cultural complexity, reducing it to an evolutionary datum. I suggest that such studies need to be qualified by reference to broader concepts so that any insights are treated on their own terms. Is it at all surprising that, in a very crude sense, patterns of human communication and behaviour mimic to some extent those found in animals? An Aristotelian philosophy would claim that it makes complete sense, but at the same time it is rash to expect such an analysis will give all the answers, for such knowledge emerges from *particular* assumptions and a *particular* way of viewing the world.

HUMAN WISDOM AND THEOLOGICAL ETHICS

Is human wisdom, as that which is connected in some sense to an understanding of God, obsolete in the light of evolutionary psychology and studies of human consciousness? This is a view endorsed by fundamentalist biologists, such as Richard Dawkins. Yet evolutionary psychology has also shown that the development of religion went hand in hand with the more advanced cultural and artistic expression that came relatively late in the evolution of our species. Religion has survival value. In this sense, I suggest that even those who do not share a particular religious belief have an interest in understanding those ancient religious traditions that served to shape earlier societies, for religion only becomes possible in more highly evolved, complex human communities. Also, even though biblical cultures are clearly distant both temporally and culturally from our present civilisation, in evolutionary time they are close, and in cosmological time even closer still. One can expect those insights that have emerged over centuries of human experience to be relevant still, for basic human needs have not changed, even if cultural expression of what those needs might entail has changed dramatically. We do not need a fixed account of 'human nature' to subscribe to this view, for human identity is capable of growth and development. In addition, this is not so much a matter of simply receiving what is given in historical texts, as appropriating those elements that are most helpful for human flourishing in our current context.

In the Hebrew Scriptures, the wisdom literature focuses on daily life and instructions for living.[12] The wisdom writers assumed that wisdom was a quality of life that humans could learn, either by experience in a family or through education. While the Torah, or law, spelt out specific instructions for how to live, wisdom writing was more open to different interpretations becoming possible in different circumstances. Human wisdom, for the Hebrew writers, was about character formation. However, it was also about human responsibility, moral integrity and accountability to God and to others, rather than individual-istic 'peak' experiences as described in the secular account of wisdom. Wisdom presupposed faith, for the fear of the Lord is the beginning of wisdom (Proverbs 1:7; 2:5; 9:10). The characters who illustrated what wisdom is like were highly diverse, from Qoheleth and his lonely journey through despair in the Book of Ecclesiastes, through to the argumentative Job, challenging his innocent suffering and the advice of conventional wisdom. Both books dealt with the dangers of conventional wisdom, in Job the idea that suffering was the result of sin, and in Ecclesiastes the dangers implicit in the obsessive search for meaning: even within the search for wisdom, the psychological danger of grandiosity becomes a striving after wind. Wisdom is 'intelligent, holy, unique, manifold, subtle, mobile, incisive, unsullied, lucid, in-vulnerable, benevolent, shrewd, irresistible, beneficent, friendly to human beings, steadfast, dependable, unperturbed, almighty, all-surveying, penetrating all intelligent, pure and most subtle spirits' (Wisdom 7:22–23). While this passage refers almost certainly to those qualities of wisdom that are divine, one can assume that those filled with the Spirit of wisdom would acquire some of these characteristics, for it is set in the context of the story about Solomon's own search for wisdom.

The wisdom literature is also replete with poetic and meta-phorical language alongside story, close observation of nature and aesthetic appreciation. The wisdom writings are an invitation to join in a story, a narrative of a particular people in their struggle to make sense of their daily lives. The Psalms present some of the most enduring examples of humanity's struggle to make sense of human experiences of celebration, community and family life, but also loss, suffering and death. Yet outside the wisdom literature there are good examples of the identification of wisdom with the Holy Spirit, in particular, that endowed on individuals for a particular task. Exodus 28:3, for example, describes those who are making the priest's garments as having the Spirit of wisdom, and the same applies to those building the tabernacle in Exodus 31:3 and 35:31. Rulers also exercise their authority in good governance through wisdom, the rule of Joseph over Egypt is successful because he is given the Spirit of wisdom (Genesis 41:38–40), and Joshua leads his people because he is full of the Spirit of wisdom (Deuteronomy 34:9; Numbers 27:18). In the New Testament, wisdom and the Spirit are associated with certain functions, so that in 1 Corinthians 12:8 the Spirit gives the gift of preaching and wisdom. Christ is also the one who endows the disciples with wisdom, as Luke 21:15 states. The real function of wisdom seems to be to guide humanity so that it acts in accordance with God's will. But wisdom as the Spirit is also capable of transforming human intentions so that they become more aligned with God's intention. In the New Testament, wisdom as a virtue becomes radicalised still further through the notion of wisdom as inclusive of suffering and even martyrdom, the wisdom of the cross.[13] As such it is dramatically counter to the culture of self-interest prescribed by evolutionary psychology. Convoluted explanations that still work on this model seem less than satisfactory.[14]

Thomas Aquinas takes up and develops the idea of wisdom as a practical basis for ethics, combining insights from the Bible, tradition and philosophy, especially that of Aristotle. For Aquinas, wisdom is one of the three intellectual virtues of speculative reason, the others being *scientia* and understanding. *Scientia* is the comprehension of the causes of things and the relationship between them, while understanding is grasping first principles. Wisdom, however, looks beyond these faculties, as it is the understanding of the fundamental causes of everything and their relationship to everything else, including God. It is, therefore, a holistic capability of human comprehension.

Aquinas followed Aristotle in suggesting that wisdom was the greatest of the intellectual virtues, but for him its ultimate authority came from its consideration of God. Yet because

Aquinas believed that complete knowledge of God is impossible, so too wisdom is always beyond human grasp. Yet even this limited form of knowledge is preferable to other forms of knowing. He believed that wisdom judges both the premises of the sciences and the conclusions that are reached by science.[15] Yet, wisdom for Aquinas was not just about giving knowledge about God in detached philosophical reasoning, but also about giving a direction to human life according to divine norms. These norms are equivalent to the divine law found in the Ten Commandments. In other words, wisdom is practically rooted as well. Aquinas thus echoes the Hebrew concept that wisdom as an intellectual virtue could be learned, but is also a gift of God.

As gift, Aquinas believed that wisdom reaches beyond the natural human capacity given in reasoning ability; it is a supernatural work of divine grace. Most contemporary philosophers and scientists resist the idea of supernatural endowments, since it implies an intrusion into the world of nature. For Aquinas the seven gifts of the Holy Spirit included *scientia* and understanding, as well as wisdom and counsel. How might a concept of grace-laden wisdom find contemporary resonance? I suggest that wisdom is graced as gift in as much as human consciousness is open to the possibility of the transcendent, ready to receive a spiritual dimension that is not only hidden, but also an integral part of the way the world is. In other words, it is not so much an intrusion of God in the world, but a discovery of God immanently present in all things. Such presence points to transcendence, but we cannot grasp such transcendence fully by human reasoning, instead we need to develop a religious and imaginative sense that is more analogous to the human experience of wonder.[16]

In this way, while one aspect of wisdom contemplates God and the nature of being in a metaphysical sense, another aspect is orientated towards action according to divine norms, for it is a participation in the divine nature by way of grace.[17] Wisdom also required the theological virtues of faith, hope and charity in order to be effective in achieving its goal. For Aquinas, wisdom is the gift of the Holy Spirit that corresponds with charity for, given the sinful nature of the human condition, conflicts are bound to arise. Love has the capacity to unite, so that wisdom is fulfilled through loving action. It is through the gifts of God's grace in faith, hope and charity that humanity becomes deified, participating in the life of God. Yet Aquinas was also keenly aware of the limitations of human knowing; God's essence is ultimately unknowable, and human minds, as created, could not know everything there is to know. In other words, humanity is capable of goodness, wisdom and charity in so far as it participates in the goodness, wisdom and charity of God.[18]

In Aquinas, wisdom as intellectual virtue of speculative reason is linked with prudence and art, which are virtues of practical reason. Prudence, or practical wisdom, is one of the four cardinal virtues, the others being justice, temperance and fortitude. Today prudence has connotations of political expediency in order to achieve particular goals. However, the classical concept of prudence was much richer than this. Aquinas suggests that wisdom teaches all four cardinal virtues, but at the same time he spoke about prudence as the servant of wisdom. Prudence and wisdom are therefore closely intermeshed as virtues. It is through prudence that humanity gains more specific guidance about how to behave ethically. The goal of all the virtues is goodness, and prudence is broadly speaking the means to reach this goal. Prudence is an act of reasoning judgement, including the steps of taking counsel, judging and then acting in a particular way. Prudence is the means through which we can decide what other virtues might mean, for example, what it means to show courage, what it means to act justly, and so on. Where the goodness being aimed at is the good of the individual, then this is individual prudence, but goodness also has a social and corporate dimension, with associated concepts of familial prudence and political prudence. How might we take counsel? This includes bearing in mind experience from the past, expressed in memory, as well as the particular circumstances of the present, and insights as to what the outcome of any decision might be. It also includes openness to being taught, understanding and reasoning. Scientific insights are therefore one facet of what it means to be prudent. Caution and foresight are also integral aspects of what it means to be prudent, but caution is not such that indecision follows, rather prudence knows when it is appropriate to take action. Prudence avoids both the danger of too hasty an action, the provision of fools in the biblical accounts, and an exaggerated timorous sense of precaution. Such a multifaceted capacity may seem complex, but prudence is just such a capacity for complex relational thinking. Prudence, as a virtue, can become a particular habit of mind. Perhaps in the light of neurological science, we can suggest that habitual use of our brain in this way will literally lead to a transformation of our minds (Ephesians 4:23).

CONCLUSIONS

I have suggested so far that human wisdom is both continuous with other forms of natural wisdom, and is also capable of expressing wisdom in a unique way. The biological basis for evolutionary continuity of humans with other creatures finds expression in neurological studies of consciousness. Creaturely consciousness is like a continuum, shading into the deepest sense of individuality and self-expression in humans. Those creatures that have relatively larger brains relative to body mass might be expected to display more complex behaviours and intelligence. Have humans evolved with their sense of consciousness and higher intelligence by accident, a chance product of the evolutionary struggle for existence, or are there restraints on the way evolution can go? I have suggested that the arguments for restraint are the most convincing, shown by some remarkable convergences in intelligence, speech, tool-making, memory and internal representations across widely different genetic lineages. While such convergences need not seem a threat (humans are not going to be taken over by super-intelligent dolphins!), at the same time, such trends should make us more humble, aware of the rich diversity of behaviours that exist in the non-human creaturely world.

Evolutionary psychologists believe that our natural craving for sugar, for example, evolved at a time when humans needed a high-energy source in order to survive. Yet it was some considerable time after the emergence of our present species, *Homo sapiens*, that we find a more sophisticated set of tools, ornaments and cultural capacities. Perhaps this was also the time when social groups became more complex, and children spent more time in playful activity. One school of evolutionary psychology argues that even those behaviours that are not directly related to biological function are passed down in an analogous way to genes; the strongest ideas are memes that are passed on to the next generation. Hence the sum of our behaviour is, for them, a combination of both our genetic and our cultural endowment, expressed as memes.

Is human wisdom a genetic endowment and a cultural meme? Human capacity for wisdom depends on prior intellectual endowment, as well as a particular nurturing environment through family and community. Yet I would resist naming wisdom as a meme except in a crude sense that something akin to wisdom has been valued across many different religious and cultural traditions. It would be more accurate, perhaps, to suggest that each society has learnt to value wisdom, but the shape of that wisdom is rooted in free action and practical projects, rather than simply received passively without alteration. Also, the extent of borrowing between different cultural expressions of wisdom depends on how far and to what extent geographical intermixing was possible. Our present global village context is very different from earlier millennia.

Yet, regardless of whether we subscribe to the memetic theory about human behaviour, the enduring existence of wisdom implies that it is worth preserving. Philosophy means the love of wisdom, and philosophers are generally sceptical about attempts to explain human behaviour through genetic, psychological, sociological or religious forms of determinism. While such explanations might give a superficial sense of security, as now a form of behaviour is 'captured', it is as illusory as Plato's image of the cave dwellers, vainly imagining that they saw reality, when all they saw were shadows on the wall. Theological interpretations of wisdom, on the other hand, at their best make fewer pretensions about explanation. Wisdom is, rather, a search to discover the inter-relationships between everything, including the search for God. Such a search is never complete, as God is not an object to be mastered by human intelligence. Wisdom in the Hebrew Scriptures is learned in a family or through education, but it also comes as a gift from God, a spiritual endowment given to humanity.

Wisdom expressed as practical wisdom or prudence is a way of thinking about how to act in an ethically responsible way. Wisdom as virtue is a habit of the mind, so disciplined to act in a way that leads to positive outcomes for the individual and the community. Such thinking might even lead to changes in neural networks, but it is a transformation that the individual chooses for him/herself, it is not simply passively received. The goal in this case is goodness, both for the individual and for the wider human community. Hence, it is not possible to say in advance what this might be, as the circumstances will change with time. Prudence also includes a cognitive skill, the ability to make decisions that take into account a complex range of factors. Yet prudence and the other virtues are not simply learned, they also include a grace-filled endowment. For it is by participation in the Goodness, Wisdom and Love of God that these virtues are realised in the human community. But what does the Wisdom of God mean? We will turn to this question in the chapter that follows.

FIVE

GOD AS WISDOM

THE NOTION THAT divinity and wisdom are intricately related to each other is an ancient one, reaching back to the earliest religious traditions before the birth of Christianity. It is, therefore, one area in which different religious traditions can find a common language, even if that language is wrapped in metaphor in rather different ways. From the perspective of evolutionary psychology, understanding what divine Wisdom means gives a window into who we are as persons, our anthropology. From the perspective of religious belief, on the other hand, reflection on divine Wisdom takes us on a journey into God, a spirituality grounded in our understanding of creation, but reaching beyond this to divine mystery. The journey will take us in two different, but complimentary directions. On the one hand, in confrontation with the reality of suffering, we are forced to reflect more deeply on who God is in the midst of such suffering. We will deal with this topic in the next chapter – the wisdom of the cross. On the other hand the journey invites us into a spirituality filled with awe and wonder, just as wonder first invited us to explore wisdom. We will deal with this topic in Chapter 7. For the time being we must be content with the foothills of what God as Wisdom might be in order to prepare ourselves for subsequent, more strenuous steps. In this chapter, I will be arguing for an understanding of God as Wisdom from an explicitly Christian perspective, laying out a trinitarian shape to that wisdom.[1]

THE COSMIC FACE OF WISDOM

(a) Hebrew wisdom

Hebrew wisdom is woven into a theology of creation; it gives an interpretation of the way God relates to the world that God has created. Wisdom in a theological sense is therefore important not just in assisting us to think more carefully about how we know what we know, but also in tracing out contours for what it means for God to be the Creator of the universe. For the sages God uses wisdom to create the world, as in Proverbs 3:13–20. Proverbs 8:22–31 takes up this theme and develops it further. It is a wonderful rendition of the work of God in creation:

> Yahweh created me, the first fruits of his fashioning, before the oldest of his works.
> From everlasting, I was firmly set, from the beginning, before the earth came into being.
> The deep was not, when I was born, not were the springs with their abounding waters.
> Before the mountains were settled, before the hills, I came to birth;
> Before he had made the earth, the countryside, and the first elements of the world.
> When he fixed the heavens firm, I was there, when he drew a circle on the surface of the deep, when he thickened the clouds above, when the sources of the deep began to swell, when he assigned the sea its boundaries – and the waters will not encroach on the shore – when he traced the foundations of the earth,
> I was beside the master craftsman, delighting him day after day, ever at play in his presence, at play everywhere on his earth, delighting to be with the children of men. (NJB)

The most usual translation of the first verse, Proverbs 8:22, is that God creates wisdom, but the Hebrew word for 'creates' more commonly means 'acquires', which implies that God gains wisdom through creative activity.[2] If we take this second translation to be correct, then this acquiring of wisdom comes very early on in the creative process, for wisdom is also named above as the 'first fruits' of God's fashioning, so that even at the very dawn of the universe, wisdom is there. The translation of Proverbs 8:30a is also ambiguous; some suggest that 'master craftsman' should be 'little child', implying that this refers to wisdom. Wisdom is at play in creation like a child. In any case, the idea that God is master craftsman separate from wisdom as implied in the New Jerusalem Bible (NJB) translation is misleading, the more correct translation should be 'I was beside him like a master craftsman.' Priestly writers also made the distinction between the work of God in *creating* and the work of God in *making*: whereas the former is unique to God, the latter has some parallels with human activity, analogous to a craftsperson in his/her particular craft. Jürgen Moltmann believes that wisdom is involved specifically in the process of making, so that 'through the art of his wisdom he shapes what he has created, giving it its life furthering form in the community of creation.'[3] This idea fits in well with other Hebrew passages, such as Wisdom 7:17, which describes the way wisdom knows about the way the world is made.

If, like Moltmann, we hold strongly to the traditional Christian view that the first creation is *out of nothing*, then subsequent acts of creation might seem to be more like a 'making' following an initial creative act. Yet, in the light of modern science, can we really distinguish so clearly between creating and making in the way that he implies, at least in this context? As the universe has unfolded, there are creative steps all along the way, and creative activity is there in both cosmic evolution and the evolution of myriad forms of life. Some theologians believe that the idea of creation out of nothing is now obsolete, so that creation is instead all a form of 'making'.[4] If we are to hold to the doctrine of creation out of nothing, we need to view it in a metaphorical way, meaning, for example, that God is the ultimate source of all being and all that exists. This is the view of Nicholas Lash.[5] He suggests that to equate God's creative activity with shaping chaos, with a 'making', is an underdeveloped doctrine of creation that is confined to the Book of Genesis. Instead, creation out of nothing is meant metaphorically to mean God as cause in the sense that God sets the *purpose* for creation. The early Patristic writers realised that rejecting *creatio ex nihilo* meant that there must be something there before God. In this case we have the problem of the source of this something, implying another force at work in distinction from God. Of course, Lash is departing somewhat from the classical tradition in Aquinas who claimed:

> Through his wisdom God is the founder of the universe of things, and we have said that in relation to them he is like an artist with regard to the things that he makes. We have also said that he is the governor of all acts and motions to be found in each and every creature. And so, as being the principle through which the universe is created, divine wisdom means art, or exemplar, or idea, and likewise it also means law, as moving all things to their divine ends.[6]

In other words, Aquinas seemed to be more than ready to speak of God as 'making' the world like an artist through wisdom. At the same time, wisdom also acts like a ruling principle in the universe in a way that gives the unfolding creation its purpose. Yet we need to be careful here, for Aquinas did not mean that God directly intervened in each and every creature, since for him God as primary cause creates through secondary causes. In the light of these reflections, can we confine wisdom to the activity of 'making' in a way that makes sense in a theology of creation? Certainly, Moltmann's initial reflections on wisdom as making seem to be extended somewhat by his later claims that wisdom is 'a creative force, it binds together the uncreated energies of God and the creative energies of what he has created. It is the divine mystery of creation, which finds expression in all created beings and their relation to each other, and yet it is more than these.'[7] The idea of wisdom as a positive transcendent energy being expressed through creation comes close to the way I see wisdom working in the universe, pointing it towards fulfilment, and giving it meaning and purpose.

Wisdom as having an 'ordering' function comes through clearly in passages such as Wisdom 7:21, which speaks of wisdom as the designer of all manner of things in the universe and on earth, from time and the seasons and movement of the stars, right through to the mental processes in humans. When Aquinas speaks about the wisdom of God in its ordering function he seems to equate this with the Eternal Law, or rationality in God, since for him 'the Eternal Law is nothing other than the exemplar of divine wisdom as directing the motions and acts of everything.'[8] Yet for Aquinas the Wisdom of God points to those truths that are *revealed truths*, not just the result of natural reasoning. In other words, we cannot arrive at an understanding of God's Wisdom simply by reflecting on the ordering in the natural world. Instead, by faith, we discern wisdom in God and then reflect on how that wisdom is operative in creation. Wisdom works holistically, from the micro through to the macro and cosmic scales. Today we might want to fill out this scope even more in the light of current scientific knowledge.

What is meant here by design? Design indicates an ordering function to wisdom. However, the Hebrews did not intend by these observations to bring people to religious faith, rather they assumed everyone who read such passages would already be a believer in a Creator God. In other words, in the light of religious belief we can say, cautiously, that God as Wisdom in some sense 'designed' the cosmos, as long as faith is presupposed, rather than becoming a primary way of leading us into faith. Of course, recognition of the intricate designs in the natural world may well reinforce that faith, but it cannot be an alternative way of finding God independent of prior revelatory experience. We need to have reached the foothills before climbing the mountain, so we need some understanding of God in faith, before we recognise God in the natural order of things. Why am I so reluctant to speak of wisdom as a form of natural theology? This reluctance rests on the history of ideas, especially in biology, for more often than not theologians have latched onto the notion of God as designer, only to find a little later more naturalistic interpretations that then evacuate the need for God.

In what sense can we begin to speak of God as Wisdom in an earth that displays a capacity to organise itself, reaching to ever more intricate expressions of complexity?[9] Life seems to express forms of complexity that are in between very ordered patterns and those devoid of such patterns. If we simply repeat a pattern, then there is little chance of novelty, whereas random change has no direction at all. There are physical and chemical constraints in evolution. However, constraints also demonstrate more elusive ways of shaping evolution towards certain end points. These constraints are known as evolutionary convergence.[10] In this context, it makes most sense to speak of the Wisdom of God acting in the process of evolution not so much in a directly causal way, but more in terms of a *presence with* the natural world as it unfolds into its rich complexity.

Some have suggested that very complex systems, such as organs like the eye, cannot have come about through contingent processes, so therefore must be 'intelligently designed'. This fits neatly with some cosmologists' understanding of a designed universe. However, it fits very poorly with what we know of biological evolution, and the way very small changes are very gradually, through a slow process of evolution, co-opted within particular constraints. A purely random process would, to put it bluntly, simply take far too long to arrive at given solutions, but there is no need to propose some sort of intelligent design to fill this gap. Instead of arguing that evolutionary design points to God, we need to presuppose that God exists, then recognise God as the active presence in the creation of life in the world, in all its richness and complexity. But does this then make a difference if God is present or not? Certainly, at one level the action of God will be completely undetectable by the tools of modern science. But theologians need not feel threatened by either this knowledge or its interpretation, unless it overreaches itself and becomes an overarching philosophy, excluding religious belief. In addition, in the eye of faith, it makes *all* the difference if God is present, for it is only within the presence of God that life can flourish, moving towards a fulfilment that is only possible in God's presence. How such flourishing can come to pass makes more sense theologically if we take account of God's activity through Christ and through the Spirit.

(b) Christ as wisdom

Classical theology traditionally viewed the way God works in the world as *Logos*, in as much as it expressed the mathematical ordering of God in creation. We then become confronted with the question of how divine Wisdom relates to the *Logos*.[11] Why is wisdom even needed if *Logos* expresses the involvement of God, more particularly the material involvement of God in the incarnation? Paul's hymn to Christ in the Letter to the Colossians 1:15–18a expresses beautifully the way Christ, the cosmic Christ, is involved in the creation of the world:

> He is the image of the unseen God,
> the first born of all creation,
> for in him were created all things
> in heaven and on earth:
> everything visible and everything invisible,
> thrones, ruling forces,
> sovereignties, powers –
> all things were created through him and for him.
> He exists before all things
> and in him all things hold together,
> and he is the Head of the Body,
> that is the church. (NJB)

Yet this hymn also connects Christ with the wisdom tradition, for it echoes expressions about the creative activity of divine Wisdom in Wisdom 7 and 8 and Proverbs 8.[12] The most likely explanation of the meaning of this passage is that the same wisdom that is at the beginning of the world also comes to find expression in Christ. The idea that Christ might also, like wisdom, be preexistent comes through more strongly in the Gospel of John. The earliest way of understanding the significance of Christ was one that expressed Christ as wisdom incarnate. The opening words of the Gospel of John, for example, speak of *Logos* as that which orders creation in a way that parallels almost exactly the role of wisdom in Proverbs. Other passages in the wisdom literature speak of wisdom as that which gives life to those who receive her, again in parallel to those passages describing Christ's role in John. Those familiar with John's Gospel would therefore tend to see the hymn in Colossians as expressing Christ as pre-existent in the creation of the world. Yet we also need to read the first half of the hymn, reproduced here, in the light of the second half, which speaks of Christ in his role as redeemer and reconciler of all things.

Given this tradition, it is hardly surprising that we find a strong identification of Christ and divine wisdom in the liturgy and tradition of the Church. In the fourth century, Constantine dedicated a cathedral church in Constantinople to Sophia (i.e. wisdom); it was rebuilt again after its destruction in 532. On entering the Cathedral of Hagia Sophia in 1994 I was immediately struck by the mosaics of Christ as *Sophia*, the architecture of the building itself representing a magnificent monument to Holy Wisdom. Yet over time in the history of the Church, the theme of Christ as *Logos* gradually took over the theme of Christ as Wisdom, the tradition of wisdom becoming obscured from view. In order to keep both traditions alive, it is important to understand the relationship between the *Logos* and wisdom, as if they become too closely identified then wisdom can all too easily simply disappear. On the other hand, the opposite danger is that wisdom no longer links into the tradition of Christ at all, becoming instead a creative principle detached from the theological tradition of the incarnation.[13] Irenaeus, for example, suggested that wisdom could be identified more with the activity of the Spirit, the *Logos* and wisdom working in parallel in creation, like two hands of God. I don't think we need to split off wisdom from the *Logos* in this way, but nor should we simply confine wisdom to the *Logos*. Perhaps it is more appropriate to see the *Logos* as just one of the movements or faces of divine wisdom.

[102]

(c) The Spirit of wisdom

The Spirit in the Hebrew Bible is often associated with its life-giving properties. However, theologians are more often than not somewhat reluctant to associate the Spirit with divine Wisdom. This may be because the Spirit is often linked with prophetic literature, whereas the wisdom literature is more 'domestic' in tone, in some sense aligned with secular traditions. Yet, just as there are passages that speak of Jesus as *Logos* in ways that parallel the wisdom literature, so there are passages that speak about the Spirit of God in a manner that reflects the Hebrew understanding of *Sophia*. In Wisdom 1:6–7 this becomes even more explicit, so 'Wisdom is a spirit ... the Spirit of the Lord, indeed, fills the whole world'.

Augustine was prepared to speak of all persons of the Trinity as being capable of expressing Wisdom. For him Wisdom in the Son and Wisdom in the Spirit expresses the wisdom of God in a similar manner to light; all three persons show the light and Wisdom of God.[14] How might we think of Wisdom in all three persons working together in the creation of the world? Moltmann names the creative action of God as like a song, and just as words require a breath to bind them all together, so 'the Creator differentiates his creatures through his creative Word and joins them through his Spirit, who is the sustainer of all his words.'[15] Given what we have said so far about wisdom, we could more explicitly name wisdom as the song of creation, but it is also a love song, love as Spirit working through the creative words of the song to achieve God's purposes for the world.

Denis Edwards coheres with this account in that he believes that we have for too long confined the workings of the Spirit to the human community, and failed to see adequately the way the Spirit of God is also the Spirit of Life.[16] His book carefully traces the biblical and Patristic tradition of God as Creator Spirit. He sees the Spirit as one who is both the midwife to the birth of the new in creation, and the faithful companion, accompanying each creature through life. Significantly, the Spirit is also the one who brings each creature into dynamic relationship with the Creator. I would agree with these notions so far, though there are some small differences. In the first place, Edwards seems to confine his understanding of wisdom to his interpretation of Christ, more specifically the *Logos*, whereas I prefer to see wisdom as also accompanying the work of the Spirit, and the work of the Father as originator of all that is. Secondly, at times he seems to veer towards a direct role of God in the course of evolution that is rather difficult to align with evolutionary explanations of novelty. For example, he suggests that:

> The Creator Spirit is not to be thought of as simply sustaining the universe, but must be thought of as enabling and empowering the genuinely new to occur. The Spirit can be understood as the immanent divine power that enables evolutionary emergence, continually giving creation itself the capacity to transcend itself and become more than it is.[17]

I am less sure how far we can attribute newness in creation to God's specific action in the world if this is understood as a form of *divine intervention*, as it implies that God is specifically most active at those times in evolution where newness unfolds in the created order. I prefer a more continuous and even sense of God actively present in the universe, a resonance of wisdom with the Spirit, a Song of creation, so that all of life is somehow caught up in God's Being. There is also a freedom implicit here as well, so that creation that deliberately turns away from participation in God no longer shares in God's life.

THE FEMININE FACE OF WISDOM

I have suggested above that we think of God working through wisdom not just in the beginning, but also through Christ in the *Logos* and through the Spirit. Hence the activity of wisdom in the Godhead is one that is trinitarian in shape. Why is it important to speak of God as Wisdom in trinitarian terms? In the first place, I think that if we confine wisdom to the *Logos*, then the richness of the tradition of Holy Wisdom becomes obscured. Secondly, if we speak in the language of the Trinity this reminds us that the activity of God in creation is both personal and relational. Philosophical accounts of the way God works in the universe can all too easily become abstract notions of God, splintering apart from the distinctive narrative features of Christian theology. In grounding Wisdom in the Trinity, Wisdom is elevated, so she is not just one way of thinking about a particular person in the Trinity, but also an integral aspect of who God is.

Of course, in speaking about God as Wisdom there is always the danger that we will be tempted to say rather too much about what this means. Moltmann believes that Sergii Bulgakov fell into this trap and he suggests that his theology of wisdom, or Sophiology is, quite simply, 'strange'.[18] But while we need to resist the idea of 'Wisdom' as a fourth person in God, a theory that Bulgakov was accused of, but subsequently rejected, we need to acknowledge that Bulgakov is a notable champion of a trinitarian understanding of wisdom. Bulgakov's ideas are also remarkably similar in many respects to the work of the highly respected Roman Catholic theologian Hans urs von Balthasar, except that in von Balthasar's case reflection on beauty or aesthetics replaces the role of wisdom, or Sophiology.[19]

What does Bulgakov say about wisdom in the Trinity in summary form? In *Sophia: The Wisdom of God*, he makes it clear that wisdom is integral to God's being (*ousia*).[20] This is, of course, a travesty of traditional Eastern Orthodox teaching that claimed that we should not speak of God's Being; rather, we can only speak of God's energies in the world. Wisdom in this scheme is one of God's energies. Bulgakov wanted to take wisdom deeper into the heart of the trinitarian life. He did, however, admit that we cannot know God as Absolute, so keeping intact the tradition of admitting that there are some things we do not know about God.[21]

What are the implications of naming Wisdom as integral to God's Being? In the first place, Wisdom is not just confined to the work of one person of the Trinity, but pervades them all. But this notion need not cause alarm, any more than does the notion that God's Love interpenetrates all persons of the trinitarian life. It also means it is possible to say a little more about God than simply that God is a mysterious essence of three persons, for the way God acts in the world becomes integral to who God is. It also means that wisdom is caught up in the work of God in salvation, as well as the work of God in creation, for wisdom marks each face of God as Trinity.

Nicholas Lash is more reserved about what we can say when it comes to speaking about God as Trinity, preferring to use the more indirect language of holiness, speech and silence.[22] Lash, on reflecting on the horror of Calvary, finds God's Word falls silent, so silence is the appropriate response of the Father. Of course, he is quite right to suggest that as we go deeper into the mystery of who God is, the more conscious we are of the depth of our unknowing. But is knowing ourselves as creatures simply a way of attending to silence? As we journey into wonder we may well experience this profound sense of silence, and I will say more about this in a later chapter, but it is also important not to resort too quickly to the notion of God as mystery. We need to stay a little longer on the foothills. In all language about God we draw on a combination of analogy and metaphor; analogy expresses ways in which God is like something we find in the world, and metaphor expresses some surprising differences. Given this qualification, then I suggest that we need to name God as both wisdom and love, for love on its own fails to express the patterned orderliness that we find in creation, and wisdom on its own fails to express the underlying movement of God towards the world, a movement of profound love. Both wisdom and love are relational affective terms; both are woven into narratives about the world and human history. Both wisdom and love point towards the ineffable in God – God's holiness.

Yet why is it so important to name wisdom as core to how we understand who God is? One reason is that wisdom comes to us as the *feminine face of God*, so that other more patriarchal images of God as Father are complemented by the image of God as feminine Wisdom.[23] Even the Orthodox writer Bulgakov spoke of wisdom as the 'eternal feminine'. Hardly surprisingly, wisdom also became associated both in the liturgical tradition and in Sophiology with the Virgin Mary. Yet by naming wisdom as integral to all three persons of the Trinity, the feminine aspect of religion could not simply be constricted to Mariology, rather the feminine reached into the heart of the Godhead. The Hebrew tradition personifies wisdom as Lady Wisdom as a foil to Folly, or the Temptress. Lady Wisdom and covenant love are spoken about together in the biblical texts, wisdom reinforcing right relationships between God and neighbour. Of course, wisdom is also associated with female goddesses in other religious traditions. The Hebrew tradition in one sense is a counter to such cults, but it also takes up the theme in distinctive ways.

Elizabeth Johnson's book *She Who Is* names God as trinitarian wisdom.[24] She renames all three persons of the Trinity in terms of *Sophia*, wisdom. Yet she is reluctant to name God the Father as *Sophia*, preferring instead Mother Sophia. Traditional orthodoxy confines the feminine in God to the third person of the Trinity, the Holy Spirit. Yet this only makes sense if the feminine is thought of as equivalent to female. In this scheme we have two male images, God as Father and God as Son, and one female image, God as Holy Spirit, who seems more amorphous and is therefore subordinated to the other two. Instead, the feminine needs to pervade all persons of the Trinity. God as Wisdom is one way of ensuring that this happens.

According to Elizabeth Johnson, God as the first person of the Trinity becomes the generative source of all that exists, the mother of the universe. There are advantages and difficulties with this kind of representation. In the first place the language of generation might lead to a view of God as 'causal agent' which then becomes problematic in the light of naturalistic explanations. We need to take care, then, not to stray into making wisdom the 'vital force' that generates the universe. On the other hand, maternal language is important in as much as it puts a correct emphasis on the intimacy between God and creation, the closeness of a caring relationship that is analogous to a mother with a child. The opposite danger to thinking of God as causal agent is to speak of God as 'final cause' or purpose in a way that seems to remove God from being caught up in human history and in the history of the cosmos. Instead, God as wisdom is present with all creation, fostering its development in particular ways, while giving creation the freedom to be itself. In this way, God as Wisdom becomes a reminder that all of life is a gift. It is experienced as a gift since everything is in a radical way contingent; it need not have been there, but it is there, for God is present with all things. The transcendence of God according to this model is not so much one of power over all things, but is hidden in profound, lasting relationships.

A way of avoiding the difficulties associated with conceiving the Wisdom in God as generative force is to see wisdom as the feminine face of God in all persons of the Trinity, including God as Father. Feminine wisdom is not so much the stereotypical pattern of the female, one who simply nurtures and gives birth to the world, but is also one who initiates, is active and is victorious over the powers of evil in the world. The identification of wisdom with the *Logos* helps to reinforce the idea of *Sophia* as the principle of rationality and order in the universe. Yet *Logos* is also the one whom John declares as incarnate in the world, the word made flesh. In this sense we can think of Jesus as Wisdom incarnate. A paradox exists between Wisdom both entering fully into the material world as Wisdom incarnate, but also being the principle of order that unfolds in the history of the universe. Hence, the transcendence of God becomes expressed both in lasting intimate relationships and in a real sense through naming God as Other than the world. In this way, transcendence also speaks of a distance between God and creation that allows God to be Lord of history, both the story of humankind and the story of the universe in all its unimaginable vastness. In other words, divine Wisdom is not just analogous to domestic wisdom found in the home and family, though it certainly is capable of expressing this intimacy, but it also declares the Wisdom of God to be profoundly different from human wisdom. This difference comes out more clearly in the Wisdom of God expressed through the cross, which we will be addressing in the next chapter.

CREATION THROUGH WISDOM

The wisdom literature of the Hebrew Scriptures is poetic and metaphorical, so similarly the way of thinking about the relationship between God as Wisdom and creation also needs to be metaphorical in tone. While we might be wary of naming God as 'cause' in a literalistic sense, God as Wisdom encourages a sense of God being in playful presence with creation as it unfolds and as one creative step follows on from another. Human wisdom is about relationships, and in an analogous way we can think of God as Wisdom being in relationship, both through reflection on the intimate relationships between Father, Son and Holy Spirit, and the relationship of all three to the unfolding of the universe. All three persons are active in creation, so in this sense it is correct to speak of creation as being through wisdom. Yet, just as wisdom describes in an intimate way what God is like, so love characterises all persons in their relationship to one another. The creation of the universe is therefore also an act of love on God's part, a joyful outflowing of the inner love of the Trinity.

St Augustine preferred to see the Holy Spirit as simply the bond of love between Father and Son. He heavily influenced the Western tradition of Christianity. However, the Eastern Orthodox tradition gave a much stronger role for the third person of the Trinity; the Holy Spirit comes out of the shadows in a way that is more distinctive when compared with Augustine's model. I prefer the Eastern notion, for it represents God in the first place as one who is in relationship; one might even add that God's being *is* communion.[25] The Eastern tradition named the inner intimacy of each person of the Trinity with itself as *perichoresis*, where each person indwells the other and acknowledges the other in relationship. Perichoresis is an idealisation of the perfection in intimacy that is only hinted at in human relationships. Yet it is helpful in as much as it represents a way of expressing both a profound intimacy, alongside a distinctiveness of persons. It represents the closest possible relationship with another, without fusing into the other. Moreover, it is through such intimacy that the distinctiveness of each person comes to light. Wisdom expresses this capacity for intimacy and distance which is difficult if we just think of God simply in terms of absolute love.

Can we think of the relationship between God and the created universe as in some sense *perichoretic*? In as much as perichoresis names intimacy and distance, this seems an appropriate way of describing poetically what the relationship between God and creation is like. I would be rather more reluctant to speak of God as having an inner *ecology*, since this might imply that God merely represents the patterns we find in life. But this does not mean that God is unconcerned about the inner relationships between all things, both in the physical world and in the life-world of dynamic, unfolding evolutionary change. God reaches into the world through indwelling, while giving an inner freedom to the world to be itself. The doctrine of the incarnation declares that God even became materially identified with the world, and in this sense affirmed the perichoretic ideal to *indwell* in the other in an even more profound identification with the natural order. The paradox of the Christian faith is that God in Christ became both human, but was also, in one sense, still divine.

How can we describe the mystery of the incarnation in terms of wisdom? Bulgakov distinguishes creaturely *Sophia*, present in the world, and divine *Sophia*, present in God. When Jesus was born, creaturely *Sophia* and divine *Sophia* met in a single person. The Virgin Mary, on the other hand, represents the fullest possible expression of creaturely *Sophia*. In her case divine *Sophia* indwelt her creaturely being through the Spirit of *Sophia*, but she is still a creature first and foremost, not divine. As applied to the creative activity of God, we can say that creaturely *Sophia* appears through the created order of the universe. It is in this sense that we can name wisdom as present in the created world, for it hints at the divine Wisdom present in God. Does creaturely *Sophia* lead us to divine *Sophia*? Such a passage implies a natural theology. However, I suggest that creaturely *Sophia* only makes sense once we reflect more profoundly on Jesus as the incarnation of divine *Sophia* in the world. It is through Christ that other forms of *Sophia* take on their meaning and significance. It is through Christ that we come to recognise what is really creaturely *Sophia* and what is her shadow. Indeed, it is from Christ that we recognise that in the Virgin Mary we find a full expression of what creaturely *Sophia* might become when transformed by divine *Sophia*.

The notion of transformation speaks of a movement in God that begins with creative activity, but is always in one sense an unfinished creation. Creation through wisdom should not imply a finished product, a static form that God then admires and declares good. Rather, the process is more fluid than this, for the intentions of God are towards transformation and eventual deification, reaching out towards what Christians have described as eternal life. But we cannot begin to understand what such transformation might mean through the Holy Spirit apart from deeper reflection on suffering in nature considered as a whole, both human and non-human alike. Such reflection takes us to a darker stage in our journey, where we contemplate the profound reality of the cross. It is through such contemplation that the meaning of creation through wisdom takes on a rather different hue. For it speaks not just of creation as ongoing energy and activity, but also of moving ahead, a journey that at once is both profoundly disturbing, but heralds a new beginning.

CONCLUSIONS

We have explored in this chapter some of the ways in which it makes sense to say that God is Wisdom. We focused particularly on the relationship between God as Wisdom and the created world, or cosmic wisdom. The Hebrew Scriptures speak in a poetic way of the role of wisdom in the creation of the world. It is important to keep this poetic stance in mind when reflecting further on the relationship between God and creation, for a more precise account of how wisdom works in the world deforms the nature of wisdom itself. Nonetheless, there are some things that we can tentatively identify as relevant. In the first place, wisdom is like a little child at play in creation, giving joy to God. Is wisdom also acting like a craftsperson, making and shaping what is there already? On the one hand, we can say that wisdom is at the border of order and chaos, helping to steer the universe to the goals hidden in the heart of God. Precisely how such steering takes place is beyond human reasoning. Yet I have suggested that we need to affirm the doctrine of creation out of nothing, even if we do not take it in a literalistic way. Why? Because the doctrine is a reminder that nothing can exist without the presence of God. Such an acknowledgement depends on faith in God, rather than exploring the workings of the world and arriving at the notion of a divine designer. God is cause in that God sustains the world in all its richness and diversity and points the universe to its future in God. However, God is not cause in the sense that God intervenes in each and every natural process.

A more helpful way of thinking about the relationship between God and creation is as indwelling presence. The Wisdom of God is arrived at through revelation, rather than in the first place from reflection on the ordering in the natural world. Such revelation permits us to look more specifically at the Wisdom of God expressed in Christ, who is also named as cosmic wisdom. Such naming identifies Christ also with the creative activity of God through wisdom. The coming of Christ is Wisdom incarnate; divine Wisdom incarnate in the material world. How are we to think of those hints of wisdom that we see in the natural order, and in human wisdom? These are best thought of as forms of creaturely wisdom that only partly reflect the divine Wisdom found in the Godhead.

The Spirit of wisdom is also there, present at the creation of the world, and engaged particularly in its journey to completion in Christ. Traditional theology has confined the feminine to the person of the Holy Spirit. I have argued, instead, that wisdom language helps to recover a sense of the feminine face of God. God is feminine not just through the Holy Spirit, but also through all persons of the Trinity. Such imagery speaks of God in intimate relationship with itself, through a divine indwelling of each person in the other. Such indwelling echoes the closeness that God comes to with creation, whispering to creation to become more fully what it is intended to be in the heart of God. And what might the intention of God be for humanity? Such intention only becomes clear paradoxically through a turn from the light to the darkness of the cross. It is to this face of wisdom that we turn in the next chapter.

SIX

CRUCIFIED WISDOM

In reaching out to explore what it means for God to be Wisdom we came across a profound mystery, that God creates the world through wisdom and love, but the natural world also suffers. What does this suffering of creation mean? Does it mean that the natural world is tainted with evil? Is it the result of a state of chaos left over at the beginning of the universe? Or is it an inevitable outcome of freedom in the natural world, without which creativity would cease? Reflection on the crucified Christ takes us deeper into the meaning of crucified wisdom. It invokes a spirituality that is not afraid to face human frailty, mortality, suffering and evil. It invokes a spirituality that connects with suffering in the natural world, including the world of human beings. It invokes a spirituality that faces cosmic physical evil. But it also invokes a spirituality that includes a dark night, a mystery of silent unknowing, which is a necessary prelude to a deeper spiritual journey into both wisdom and wonder.

SUFFERING IN NATURE

Suffering in nature is normally associated with the ability to feel pain, so suffering would only be identified with creatures that have some sort of neural networks. Among sentient creatures we find countless stories of suffering through predation and para-sitism, so graphically illustrated by Annie Dillard's account of the frog being liquidised by a predatory beetle. Those with more developed neural pathways also have the capacity to feel intense fear associated with impending suffering and death. Human suffering reaches particular intensity through humanity's atrocious acts towards its own species, including not just physical torture and killing, but also psychological torment as well. This is different from dying of old age, even though this too brings its share of suffering. Mortality, though, is an aspect of biological life that is related to the second law of thermodynamics and an inbuilt lifespan appropriate for any given species.[1] Yet we can also widen the definition of suffering to include annihilation, for even if a creature cannot feel pain, a loss of that species is a genuine loss of potentiality, a life that has come so far in the billions of years of evolution only to be snuffed out and extinguished. Such suffering may be related to human activity, but evolutionary science also tells a grim story of mass extinctions even before humans appeared. Millions upon millions of species have simply disappeared. The fossil record tells of an explosion of life forms in the Cambrian Period some 500 or so million years ago. However, the record also provides evidence for mass extinctions; about 250 million years ago 90 per cent of marine species disappeared, some 65 million years ago more than half of all the species on earth were lost, including dinosaurs. Mammals could not have flourished unless dinosaurs had been erased from evolution. The earth only houses about 2 per cent of the species that have ever come into existence. Such wastage also seems to be an echo of the story of the beginning of the cosmos, where almost all matter ends up in radiation, and what is left explodes into supernova. Very early life forms became quashed soon after they had begun, until eventually the conditions became right for life to continue.

What is the human response to such rampant suffering? Certainly, humanity has only become aware of the extent and intensity of the suffering in the living world relatively recently in human history. We cannot simply explain it by linking such suffering with human sinfulness according to the Fall of Adam and Eve in a traditional theological exposition. How far is such suffering and waste compatible with belief in a good God who has declared all creation to be good? This deepens the problem that Christians have struggled to come to terms with for centuries, namely how to explain the existence of suffering alongside belief in a good Creator. Traditional theories focused on the notion of freedom – that without suffering there could be no intense happiness and freedom to choose between good and evil. The so-called free will defence is more successful in explaining *moral evil*, rather than amoral, natural evil. The difference that evolutionary suffering makes in this case is that it seems to impinge on the fabric of the way the world has come into existence. Could a good creative God, in other words, really endorse or even be intimately involved with a process that leads to so much pain and suffering? When does such suffering become positively *evil*, or is evil only ever associated with free moral choice on the part of humans? The conventional wisdom of Job's counsellors was that his personal suffering was a result or outcome of evil actions on the part of human beings. Jesus also accepted this philosophy in part, though he was able to distinguish between those situations where suffering was a consequence of evil deeds, and those situations where suffering was just there as a result of 'natural' inheritance.[2] We also need to distinguish between moral evil and amoral evil, which arises through what we might see as cruel or injurious events. The boundaries between evil and suffering are becoming even more blurred in contemporary culture. If morally evil actions follow spontaneously from 'natural' causes, such as mental health problems, then suffering includes the propensity to do moral evil. In such cases the community has a responsibility to protect the individual from self-harm or harm to others. Deeper understanding of human psychology has gradually eroded those behaviours considered morally 'evil'; they become, instead, outcomes of particular aspects of human physical, mental or social suffering. On the other hand, the extent of suffering in nature alongside natural disasters raises the question of nature being evil in the amoral sense, rather than good.[3] A modified version of the free will defence is that the inherent creativity in nature requires such suffering if it is to genuinely explore the different options set before it. Yet such logical defence begins to crumble once we face more deeply the extent of suffering discovered in the natural and human world.

[115]

Reflection on the origin of evil in the classical period permitted the emergence of all kinds of dualistic philosophies, that is, ways of separating out the good and the evil into two different realms. If, as the Manicheans maintained, the material world is designated evil, then finding any goodness within it comes more as a surprise, for goodness is only attributed to the spiritual, immortal realm. In such a way death is associated with an evil, finite, material world. But the early Christian Fathers rejected such explanations, for it implied that God had created an evil world, counter to the teaching in the Book of Genesis. It was one reason why the concept of creation out of nothing came to prominence, for if all creation has its origin in God, then no material thing can be evil in the sense of being an absolute force in opposition to God. Remnants of Manicheanism remain in contemporary theories about the origin of evil. Sjoerd Bonting, for example, suggests that evil is directly related to the chaos that has existed at the beginning of the creation of the world, dismissing as obsolete the notion of *creatio ex nihilo*, creation out of nothing.[4] His theory is far more sophisticated than a simple dualism of a good ethereal world and an evil material world, for in his case he speaks of chaos as being an evil *state* of matter, rather than being associated with materiality as such.[5] His scheme also has the advantage of associating creative activity in the material, ordered world with God. He manages in this way to avoid the Gnostic heresy that claims the material world is evil. However, his admission of chaos as being in some sense 'outside' God's control permits a dualism in states of matter whereby some states of matter are opposed to God and some are not thus opposed.

But what might be the reason for his optimism that such chaos will be overcome in the final victory, if such chaos is beyond God's power in the beginning? Has the escape of chaos from the remit of that which God contains solved one problem, but once more reintroduced that terror of empty space which Pascal saw so passionately? For the vastness of the universe led Pascal to exclaim that 'the eternal silence of these infinite spaces terrifies me'.[6] The idea of such primeval chaos existing since the beginning from an origin that is wholly unknown can serve to reinforce such terror. However attractive such dualistic ideas might be in order to help us come to terms with suffering alongside notions of a good God, ultimately they are unsatisfactory, for they fail to render God as Creator of all creation, and thus undermine the hope in the future of that creation. But the dilemma is that if, instead, God is the author even of such chaos, then how do we deal with suffering in nature, understood as including humanity?

THE WISDOM OF THE CROSS

We can think of the whole of evolutionary history being caught up into Christ, as Christ is one who enters into the heart of the evolutionary process, being present with all biological life in what we might care to term a *deep incarnation*.[7] Yet at the same time, Christ also has the capacity to suffer with and redeem all of creation. Reflection on the cross of Christ is not so much a philosophical solution to the problem of evil and suffering, as a way of coming to terms with it theologically and spiritually. Awareness of suffering and, some might add, evil in the natural world, independent of human activity, adds another dimension to such reflection. For now the suffering in Christ does not just come alongside human suffering, but is also in kinship with the suffering of all living creatures. In as much as the evolving cosmos speaks of broken possibilities then the crucified Christ also speaks to such situations of brokenness as well. Above all, the crucified Christ is a way of taking pain and suffering into the heart of who God is, rather than separating out such suffering and pain from the intentions of God.[8]

But what does it mean, specifically, to speak of the *Wisdom* of the cross?[9] In the last chapter I suggested that divine Wisdom is present in all three persons of the Trinity in particular ways. Wisdom in Christ comes in the form of Wisdom incarnate, divine Wisdom appearing in the form of a human being, the man Jesus. Hence, just as Jesus is crucified, so it makes sense to speak of crucified Wisdom. The idea of associating the positive notion of wisdom with crucifixion can be somewhat shocking. Consider for a moment the humiliating and demeaning torture that crucifixion is: the physical pain and suffering is almost indescribable. Alongside this claim is the idea that, for Jesus at least, the experience of crucifixion included a feeling of total and terrible separation from God, culminating in the agonised cry, 'My God, my God, why have you forsaken me?' The fear of such separation accounted for his deep wrestling in the Garden of Gethsemane, for it was not just the physical suffering that he dreaded, but rather being abandoned by God to his terrible fate. How can this possibly be a feature of divine Wisdom, if wisdom is primarily about interrelationship and indwelling, for it seems to fly in the face of such interpretation?

For the apostle Paul, writing in the First Letter to the Corinthians, Chapter 1, the Wisdom of the cross is not just unable to quench the Wisdom of God, rather, even more remarkably perhaps, *the Wisdom of the cross is the Wisdom of God.* Perhaps we should note the specific context in which Paul was writing here, namely the boastful arrogance of this Christian community, engaged in bitter rivalry against one another, each convinced of their own superior rhetorical eloquence. His claim turns such arrogant jockeying upside down, for the Wisdom of the cross inverts the Wisdom of the world. Paul's insistence on the Wisdom of the cross is a direct counter to Gnostic tendencies, which claimed that it was possible to arrive at forms of superior knowledge in detachment from the material, suffering world. Instead, the Wisdom of the cross announces God's radical involvement with that suffering. Paul was resisting an over-reliance on human wisdom, judgement and ability to understand. Instead, he wanted his readers to be confronted with the mystery of the cross. Above all, Paul insisted that God works with those whom the world believed to be 'foolish', those people wrongly considered by others as highly unlikely to receive God's favour. Why? God works with those who are considered weak or foolish in the world in order to bring shame on those who think themselves wise.

Did Paul also mean that Jesus in some way fulfilled the teaching of Torah, considered by some wisdom books to be identified with wisdom? Or perhaps he was simply using the language of his

Gnostic opponents in an ironic way by referring to Christ as Wisdom. More likely, however, is that Paul is deliberately linking divine Wisdom with God's righteousness, sanctification and redemption (1 Corinthians 1:30). This links wisdom with themes of salvation, hence naming the cross of Christ as part of the history of salvation. The cross expresses the extent of God's love for creation and God's willingness to suffer for the sake of creation. Crucified wisdom represents the inner dimension of pain taken into the heart of God's self-knowledge. Holmes Rolston talks about the suffering of nature as being cruciform.[10] By this he means that the whole of nature also reflects the character of God as the Suffering Redeemer, so that while species do die and go extinct, they are always transformed into something else. So, 'There is something divine about the power to suffer through to something higher ... The cruciform creation is, in the end, deiform, godly, just because of this element of struggle, not in spite of it. There is a great divine "yes" hidden behind and within every "no" of crushing nature.'[11]

There are two aspects to this issue that we need to hold in tension with each other. In the first place, just as there is ultimately no possible answer to Jesus' cry of dereliction, Why have you forsaken me?, so there is no pat theological answer to the question, Why so much natural suffering and evil?, even if it is possible to account for such suffering by naturalistic interpretations according to the theory of evolution. For once we try and explain such suffering, then it might seem to become a *necessary* part of the process of redeemed creativity. Crucified Wisdom does *not* mean that the cross was an inevitable aspect or principle of creation in the manner implied by Holmes Rolston above, even though at first sight this seems an attractive way of integrating Christ with the suffering of creation. If this were really the case it would make God out to be a monster; one who deliberately punished Christ on the cross for the sake of the resurrection; or one who deliberately punishes the natural order in amoral evil for the sake of an evolutionary future. In the second place, on the other hand, the suffering of Christ on the cross and the suffering of the natural order is not the final word in salvation history. Although the mystery of why such suffering occurs remains, we need to hold this in tension with the Christian hope that Christ was not simply crucified, but he also experienced resurrection from the dead.

What does it mean to acknowledge the presence of God's grace in the midst of suffering? The Wisdom of the cross, according to this account, becomes infused with divine grace and glory. For John's Gospel the cross is not simply the site of humiliation and disgrace, but also where the glory of God shines through. Such glory comes from knowing Christ to be pre-existent Wisdom, but also because of the future hope embedded in the resurrection account. Ultimately the Christian message is not one that ends with crucifixion in isolation, but also reflects back in the light of hope in the resurrection. This means that when we reflect on the suffering of the natural world its own suffering is taken up into the suffering of Christ, but not in the sense of hopeless, meaningless suffering, for such suffering is not apart from God's presence.

Christ as one who suffers does not serve to initiate a principle in creation. Rather, Christ, on the cross, demonstrates clearly that the love of God is a vulnerable, self-limiting love. It is love that is vulnerable because Christ experiences himself as abandoned, hanging naked on the cross, open to human derision. It is a love that is self-limiting, self-emptying, some say *kenotic*, because it could have been otherwise, and Christ empties himself of any Godlike power in order to take on the form of a slave (Philippians 2:7). This giving up of power for the sake of demonstrating a love beyond human imagining is a crucial element of the Wisdom of the cross. Wisdom that is false seeks forms of power over others, but the wisdom that comes from God, crucified Wisdom, *identifies with the powerless and weak*. By giving up power in this way, the freedom of the other becomes assured, for it makes room for the other to be itself. Denis Edwards argues, therefore, that 'Only a God whose power is absolute, unconditioned and arbitrary would always be completely free to intervene to stop a tidal wave or ensure that a dangerous mutation did not occur.'[12] In addition, when speaking of a God who suffers this does not mean God is the same as the finite world, for God's capacity to feel is infinitely greater than that possible for finite creatures. Crucified Wisdom brings pain to the depths of the trinitarian life, but such pain is *analogous* to pain found in the created order; to say otherwise would be to equate God with the world.

THE REDEMPTION OF NATURE

What is the relationship between Christ, creation and redemption? The analogy between Christ and the figure of Wisdom in the creation of the world in Paul's Letter to the Colossians hints at Christ's identification with wisdom.[13] However, the remainder of the poem is also important, since it leads on to a fuller discussion of the redeeming work of Christ in creation:

> He is the Beginning, the first-born from the dead,
> So that he should be supreme in every way;
> Because God wanted all fullness to be found in him,
> And through him to reconcile all things to him,
> Everything in heaven and everything on earth,
> By making peace through his death on the cross.
>
> *Colossians 1:18b–20* (NJB)

This text speaks of Christ as being the mediator of redemption, reconciling *all things*, meaning the entire created universe. Colossians 1:16 also declares Christ as head of the church and 1:20 speaks of the cross, both of which are added to the original hymn to wisdom. Some commentators believe that, in the light of the additions to the text, 'all things' means just the Christian community, but this seems to empty the poem of its original reference to *cosmic* wisdom. Although some biblical scholars resist interpreting these verses as indicating a cosmic redemption, it strikes me as anthropocentric to assume that cosmic redemption is not implied. If Hebrew wisdom was thought of in terms of cosmic creation and salvation, then Christ crucified is likely to go beyond relevance confined to the human community. But the movement in these verses is one of *reconciliation*, a process that seeks to go beyond creativity as such to the redemption of the suffering inherent in that creative process.

The vision of the kingdom of God in Isaiah was one of a peace-able kingdom, where the lion would lay down with the lamb in what might be thought of as an 'unnatural' reconciliation. Prior to reconciliation is a disruption to the ideal state of harmony, but rarefying the natural world in idealised harmonious terms misses out important aspects of vulnerable, creaturely existence.

In Chapter 8 of his Letter to the Romans, Paul speaks of a groaning of all creation, waiting for redemption. This is unlikely to refer to the sufferings of Christ, but is more likely to express the sharing of the suffering of the Holy Spirit in the painful experiences of creation, a coming to birth. Denis Edwards expresses the same hope in his suggestion that 'The Spirit can be thought of as the midwife who helps creation in its travail as it brings the new to birth.'[14] The activity of the Spirit is one engaged in the evolutionary creation of the new. Given our under-standing of the extent of suffering in the creative evolution of the natural world, does it make more sense now to consider creation and redemption as integrated interrelated processes, rather than creation being in some sense prior to redemption? My response to this is both yes and no. Yes, there is a sense in which redemp-tion is inherent in creativity in as much as the suffering of the world connects with the suffering of Christ and the Spirit. In as much as the creation co-suffers with Christ through the Spirit it also shares in Christ's redemptive work towards a new creation that begins in this world. Yet on the other hand, the Spirit's creative suffering is a groaning, a waiting for redemption, and an anticipation of future hope, a new creation that has yet to be fully revealed.

Why does the Spirit of God suffer with creation as it awaits the redemption of the world? Such suffering of the Spirit, like the suffering of Christ, is not a *necessary* suffering, but out of the freedom of divine love. In other words, 'This kind of suffering springs from the incomprehensible depths of divine compassion. The Spirit suffers with creation not to glorify suffering, but in order to bring liberation and healing.'[15] Hence, hints at the new creation are a foretaste of what is to come, where reconciliation will finally come about in the new heaven and the new earth. This represents a new order of reality, a new creation, even if it still draws on what has been found in present created reality.

Can the extent of divine compassion extend to every individual creature in evolutionary history, so that all creatures are redeemed? Denis Edwards believes that we can still hold to the traditional belief that God cares for every creature by reflecting more deeply on the significance of Christ's death and resurrection.[16] If all creatures that have been annihilated through evolutionary processes are still loved by God, then we can view them as victims of evolution. Jürgen Moltmann views the future kingdom of God breaking into the present and past, so that all things, including the victims of evolution, experience the new creation 'simultaneously' when time ends.[17] He reinforces the idea of Christ coming to renew all things in his later work, so 'consummation brings back everything that had ever been before'.[18] The plenitude of the new creation is not simply the rational outcome of God's will, or a means of God's self-realisation, but is also a feast of God's eternal joy, stemming from the Easter event.[19]

Such an optimistic view of all of life from all times and all spaces being gathered up into God stretches human imagination almost to breaking point. Process thought, following Alfred North Whitehead, adopts a far more modest view. Whitehead argued that creatures have a permanent effect on God's consequent nature. Of course, this seems an unsatisfying version of the resurrection in that when I die I would have no awareness of having influenced God in this way, so what might be the point of such hope, apart from a vague belief that I have somehow influenced God? Ian Barbour modifies this view so that individual subjective experience continues, but this could only reasonably be applied to those with subjectivity.[20] Ernst Conradie's idea of material inscription is interesting, as he claims that the history of the cosmos is somehow inscribed into dimensions of space and time.[21] The events of the past are somehow inscribed into these dimensions, but also open to the possibility of healing.

Denis Edwards builds on this latter view in a fascinating way.[22] He makes five points. First, the future of the universe remains obscure and surrounded in mystery. All we have in the resurrection of Jesus is a promise, based on what we know already of the character of God. Second, individual creatures are inscribed in the eternal divine life through the Holy Spirit. But he does not view such inscription as simply the eternal memory of an idea, but much more positively, in terms of embodiment. Third, the healing and fulfilment of creatures comes from the crucified Christ. Fourth, redemption of creatures will be specific for each creaturely being, so that 'Based upon God's wisdom and justice, I believe that it can be taken as a fundamental principle that redemptive fulfilment of any creature will be specific to the creature involved.'[23] Fifth, some individual creatures may find redemption in the living memory and the eternal life of the Trinity and the communion of saints. While human beings can hope for an embodied resurrection, what is appropriate for a mosquito or individual dinosaur? A hope for the ongoing fellowship of life of other creatures draws on the tradition of communion as celebrated in the Eucharist.

I think that Edwards's approach to the redeemed life of creation is helpful in that it avoids both the problems associated with process theology's minimalist account of the resurrection and some of the difficulties in conceiving Moltmann's much more lavish account. Yet I also think we need to include one caveat to this very reasonable account, and this caveat is based on further reflection on crucified Wisdom. Such wisdom has taught us that our notions of power are mistaken, that God comes in the form of slave and servant, turning upside down our notions of what God is like. In much the same way, I suggest that there will almost certainly be plenty of surprises in heaven. What might seem to us to be a species worthy of individual inclusion in the bodily resurrection of life may turn out not to be the case. Of course, if a creature has no consciousness then there would seem to be less point to an individual resurrection, a treasured memory inscribed into the heart of God may well be sufficient. But if this is the case, then how can we also experience communion with such creatures, unless, as Edwards implies, human beings also somehow share something of the delight of the divine persons in treasuring the memory of each and every creature? Perhaps part of the joy we experience in heaven is the joy of communion, not just with creatures like ourselves, but also somehow with all creatures in their varied evolutionary history on earth. In any case, redeemed creation will have myriad possibilities for interaction and communion.

The Book of Proverbs 9:5 speaks of wisdom's banquet, sharing in her wine and her bread with those who seek after her. This connects directly with Jesus' self-portrait in John 6:27, where he describes himself as the bread of life. It also, significantly, connects with Jesus' identification of himself with bread and wine in the Eucharistic feast. The connection between Jesus and wisdom's banquet comes through clearly in some of the architecture and iconography of the early church. Proverbs 9:6 speaks of those who follow her as capable of walking in the way of perception. Paul takes up this idea in the Letter to the Ephesians, so that wisdom and understanding come to those who are united in Christ's death (Ephesians 1:7–8), expressing a final hope that all things in heaven and on earth will be brought together under one head, namely Christ (Ephesians 1:10). The relationship between the banquet of wisdom and the Eucharist is also important for another reason, namely that it keeps the idea of metaphorical theology alive. Visions of the future for creation need, necessarily, to be metaphorical accounts based on what we know of this universe. It is here that language comes up against its limits, moving into a mysticism that I will come back to again in the section below and in the next chapter. The danger, of course, of thinking of the new creation in mystical terms is that human responsibility towards this earth will be weakened. The challenge is to be modest in our formulations based on our experiential knowledge of God, but at the same time be aware of the ethical implications of particular positions. A removal of creation into a mystical, unknown future could alleviate human responsibility as much as a description of a radically new creation in concrete terms.

What about the future of the universe as portrayed by modern physicists? John Polkinghorne has written passionately about this topic, given his familiarity with the future of the universe according to physical theories, and his own deep commitment to Christian faith.[24] Physicists predict that in 5 billion or so years time the sun will have run out of hydrogen, swelling to become a red giant that would fry any remaining life existing on earth. On an even longer timescale the universe will either implode in a 'big crunch', or expand, eventually degrading into radiation. From a cosmologist's point of view, the fate of the universe is ultimately futile. Polkinghorne argues, instead, that the new creation will be genuinely new, including new laws that are appropriate to its nature, but continuity comes from transformation of the natural world that exists now.[25] He also believes that the new creation, freed from its tendencies for sin, will enter into the dynamic life of the Trinity. The old creation is like a 'raw material' for the new, including its new combination of 'space', 'time' and 'matter'. His idea that there will be time in the new creation, that human life will be in some sense temporal as well as in some sense embodied, offers a view of the future world that is everlasting, rather than a timeless world of 'eternity'. The way the old intersects with the new is, for him, an information-mapping process between different dimensions of the divinely sustained reality. According to this view, time will converge on the 'time' of the new creation, so that the experience will be one of simultaneous resurrection. Polkinghorne also resists the idea that all living creatures will have their own individual eschatological future, while wanting to preserve a memory of creatures, redeemed in such a way that they are no longer predatory.[26]

Polkinghorne's idea that there will be laws in the new creation of a different type compared with those that exist in the present universe certainly makes sense. Ephesians speaks of Christ's powers of reconciliation that extend to disarming of negative cosmic forces (Ephesians 1:21). This might imply redemption of physical laws which, according to modern physics, are inevitably locked into a process of decay and final annihilation. Yet I would also want to add that it is quite possible that the new creation that Polkinghorne speaks about exists in some kind of parallel universe to our own, even now, rather than waiting for the final resurrection. It is true that at the second coming of Christ some sea change will occur, so that life as it is known on earth will in some sense cease to exist. But the resurrection of Christ also promises a taste of the kingdom of God now, as well as a future one. Some experience of what this life might be like can also be experienced now in this life, which is why it makes sense to ask the saints to pray for us. If they were simply in a suspended state, waiting for the final resurrection, then any sense of communion with those who have died is meaningless. The tradition of the communion with the saints is stronger in the Roman Catholic and Orthodox traditions, so belief in such a possibility is not universal.

CRUCIFIED WISDOM AND THE
VALUE OF NATURE

What are the implications of considering God's Wisdom as also crucified Wisdom? In the first place, as I hinted earlier, it qualifies any sense of our own sense of superiority over and above other creatures. Human wisdom can learn from creatures that are not like us. In the second place, it invites humanity to share in the suffering of the world through imitation of Christ. We are called to carry the cross with Christ daily, not just intermittently. Just as the scope of Christ's suffering and redemption is in some sense inclusive of all creaturely suffering, so we are challenged to move not just beyond our kin to share in the suffering of those within the human community, but also to begin to take account of the suffering of non-human creatures as well. Of course, it is much easier for us to identify with those creatures that are more like ourselves, or who have had a relationship with human communities through domestication or friendship.

In Britain the tradition of love for animals has a long history, one that is not so much romantic in its attachment to non-humans, but takes due regard of animal welfare and animal suffering.[27] Veterinary science grew up in order to care for those animals that are associated with the human community. Even the most anthropocentric attitude to animals is forced to respect a minimal standard of care. The spread of avian flu across to the human species, the spread of 'mad cow disease', and even the spread of AIDS, thought to have originated in a primate population, reinforces the wisdom of caring not just for our own species, but for other species as well. Yet crucified Wisdom, because it is *cosmic* in scope, invites a more profound level of caring that demonstrates *agape*, or loving regard for our neighbour, including our creaturely non-human neighbours. This means that destruction of habitats, the slow loss of biodiversity and the loss of myriad species that humanity has not even identified, is a real loss, a suffering that humanity is called to embrace and resist, even if it is to the disadvantage of human life. I choose these words with care, for we cannot weigh in the balance the loss of human life relative to the life of an animal. Animal rights do not, therefore, extend to the extent that their lives have to be preserved even if this means that life-saving treatment for dying humans is withdrawn. But any such sacrifices need to be seen as less than ideal and examples of our own broken condition prior to the new creation.

Do animals also share in the experience of the crucified one; in other words, can dolphins also carry the cross?[28] Michael Northcott makes this provocative suggestion in the context of considering how far and to what extent dolphins are also caught up in the story of redemption. Are dolphins caught up in this story not just through suffering from disease, but also because of some willed action on their part that prevents their flourishing? This might arise, perhaps, through fighting wars with other dolphin groups, or becoming addicted to destructive behaviour, or rejecting their responsibilities as parents. He believes that dolphins do this, but to a much lesser extent than human societies and some other social species. In this sense they also stand in need of redemption, as well as deliverance from other forms of suffering. But they do not carry the cross in the sense of being able to share in the concept of God. They do reveal the cross in as much as they show the moral priority of the weak, and give us examples of vulnerable care and dependence, living richly exuberant, communicative, intelligent and playful lives. Fortunately Northcott does not take the next step and argue that such moral priority means that intelligent animals have a status even above that of human children.[29] Yet one might want to hold back from Northcott's endorsement of the 'cruciformity' of the cosmos as a *realist* narrative, for it might seem to encourage a view of suffering as a fundamental principle of being, rather than seeing the cross as radically contingent, as I discussed earlier. The cosmos is only cruciform in as much as its suffering is not excluded from that of Christ. However, we can, with Northcott, affirm the value of the dolphin world as one that points in a rich way to what the new creation may be like. It also challenges our ethical treatment of these wonderful creatures.

Can we take this further and suggest, with Christopher Southgate, that humanity is *also* called to share in the redemption of the creaturely world?[30] This is certainly a bold suggestion, going even beyond the notion of humanity as co-creator. Yet I would hesitate to endorse this, for our experience of assisting redemption in the human species has been one of profound failure. It also tends to reinforce the notion of our own power and superiority, in opposition to the Wisdom of the cross. I would prefer to see the need for human redemption from sin, which is the sin of neglect or more active abuse of the natural world. Southgate does not seem to mean by co-redemption 'improving' nature, but rather 'holding back from mass extinctions'. But this sounds more like redemption *from sin*, rather than co-redemption *of nature*.

Crucified wisdom also paradoxically points to the value of all life, but also its limitation. In other words, it helps us to face up to creaturely finitude. One of the trends in human societies is towards a greater and greater resistance to the fact of our own mortality. Medical science in Western society often seems bent on avoiding the issue, prolonging human life in a seeming desperation to avoid the moment of death. Euthanasia is a counter reaction to such a trend, but euthanasia expresses more commonly another form of avoidance, namely the avoidance of suffering associated with dying. Another trend is a resistance to all forms of imperfection: the social exclusion of those who are different or who fail to live up to our own preconceived conceptions of a fulfilled and healthy life. The Wisdom of the cross takes the most shameful imaginable human suffering, exclusion and death and eventually turns it into a temple of glory. However, the Wisdom of the cross is also about an entering into a dark existential space where meaning seemingly disappears. All suffering and death is anticipated in this way, for it is a lonely confrontation with an unknown future.

Nicholas Lash suggests that death is not, in itself, disastrous, though I would contend that culturally it is often viewed as such.[31] Lash invites us to consider not just death, but disaster, a disaster that effectively silences our speech. Such disasters include the sheer scale of suffering experienced by human beings towards each other through genocide. He does not mention the suffering experienced by the annihilation of millions of species, but this, to my mind at least, would qualify as a disaster that has the potential, at least, to silence speech. He traces Christ's cry of dereliction from the cross to the Psalm of its origin, where the Psalmist speaks about the watery chaos at the beginning of the world. In this way, 'In Jesus' dying, the Word that makes and orders all the things there are is itself threatened by the chaos-waters which were, "in the beginning", by that Word set in their place.' Hence, 'the pain and darkness of the world go right down to the very heart of things, silencing God's own speech, and yet, in that dreadful silence, the world is made again, there is a new creation.'[32] As Jesus articulated in agonised anticipation his own dying, the response he heard was one of silence. He therefore argues that it is inappropriate to expect much more, so that, 'the more we begin to gain something of the holy mystery of God, the more that what we are and what we say and what we do refracts the character of God's Word, the more conscious we become of the depths of our unknowing. God becomes more unknown, not less the more we understand him.'[33] The Wisdom of the cross is another reminder of this mystery, for this 'foolishness' became the means for cosmic redemption.

CONCLUSIONS

I began this chapter by reflecting on the extent of suffering and the sheer scale of the evolutionary loss of species, and what one might call amoral evil, existing in the natural world. But such devastation needn't push us into the ancient belief that evil is a separate force from God, however tempting such a solution may seem as a comfort in our struggle to find meaning. Instead, the Wisdom of the cross serves to confront us with the notion that the Wisdom of God is also the Wisdom of the cross. Such wisdom works on a number of different levels. In the first place it challenges any sense of human superiority of knowledge or arrogance on our part. In the second place, the cross connects with the history of salvation, not just for humanity, but in a wider, cosmic sense as well.

Is nature in some sense cruciform? If by this we mean that the suffering in the entire natural world is somehow taken up into Christ's suffering, then the answer to this is yes. But it does not mean that the cross is a principle of the natural world, as if this were the case then Christ's suffering and that of all of living nature would somehow be necessary. Wisdom, instead, revolutionises the notion of power. The Spirit groans with all of creation in its birth, but also in its redemption. How should we conceive creaturely redemption? Are creatures somehow inscribed into God's memory? I argued that this view needs supplementing with a stronger sense of individual participation, the nature of which we might only guess. The language in which we describe the new creation needs to be metaphorical, for its newness means that time, space and matter will be radically transformed, entering perhaps new dimensions of reality. The implications of such reflections are that humanity is called to serve the community of creation, rather than dominate it for its own ends and purposes. Further, we need to learn from the life of other creaturely beings, and be prepared to acknowledge that the redeeming work of Christ is present to creatures other than humankind. Finally, reflection on the cross of Christ takes us into a dark night of the

[131]

soul, one where we are confronted by a profound silence. What is beyond this silence? For Lash it is the deeper strangeness of grace. It is to this experience of God's grace set in the context of the natural world in all its fecundity and contingency that we turn in the chapter that follows.

The stranger on the road to Emmaus gives the disciples a new sense about what had happened in his own story. I would contend that in the light of faith, this newness could also apply to the way we perceive the cosmos. But it is a view that is also fully aware that the one who teaches us is the crucified one, who still bears on his hands and feet the marks of the crucifixion. Crucified Wisdom remains hidden in the Wisdom of God, even as we journey towards that wisdom in wonder.

SEVEN

JOURNEY INTO WONDER

Wonder in the natural world gives us a direct experience of what it is to wonder. Such experiences can, in some cases, lead to a sense of the transcendent, an experience of religious awe rather like that portrayed through landscape painting and abstract art.[1] A similar, though more scientific, experience of wonder comes from paying close attention to the natural world through observation of the stars or natural history, as I have suggested in earlier chapters. More detailed scientific investigation of the cosmos and life around us through the tools of physics and experimental science may also lead to an indirect sense of wonder. As we think of some of the amazing discoveries of cosmology and evolutionary science, we are soon caught up in a mood of astonished wonder. When such experiences are related to a sense of the divine, then we may find challenges to our preconceived ideas about the divine. Most scientists would want their religious beliefs to be compatible, at least, with their discoveries about the natural world. In a post-modern culture the very possibility of such a challenge is thwarted, for post-modernity in its more radical form assumes a philosophy of construction, that humanity literally makes its own worlds. The experience of wonder in the natural world in both a direct or indirect sense challenges such a notion, for wonder connotes the unexpected, the surprise that seems to take us out of ourselves into another realm. How far are such experiences valid from a specifically religious point of view? Certainly, theologians would want to test such experiences against the tradition, rather than the other way round. But such experiences are helpful in as much as they open up the possibility of God's existence, even if we might draw back from saying that they tell us more assuredly what God is like.

Systematic theology might also take us towards a sense of wonder in our understanding of God and who God is in the world today. Yet the enchantment that we might feel in the natural world, either indirectly or directly, and the wonder experienced as we begin to explore what God is like, soon becomes challenged by human suffering akin to all natural suffering. It is as if the journey into wonder has bumped up against an impossible challenge, confronted as we are by the additional image of God as crucified Wisdom. Yet my suggestion in the last chapter is that such reflection on Christ is a necessary prelude for a deeper ascent. The movement in Christian spirituality is one of ascent, descent, and then ascent.[2] If we miss out the descent aspect, then our ascent becomes shallow, even if the value of direct experience of the divine in the natural world consists in showing the possibility of the sacramental presence of God throughout the world.[3]

WONDER IN THE NEW TESTAMENT

The experience of wonder is one documented in both the Hebrew Bible and the New Testament. It comes to the surface in the Gospel accounts of Jesus' life and ministry, and also in the Acts of the Apostles. Perhaps the way wonder is used in these texts can show us more clearly the value of wonder today and take us a little further on our journey into wonder. What was the background to the notion of wonder in the New Testament?[4] In the Greco-Roman literature of the period, writers used wonder in order to indicate divine acts or interventions by gods. The historian Philo linked reactions of wonder to dreams, to divine epiphanies, to virtues of particular individuals and to the law. Josephus, on the other hand, linked wonder with miracles, war, portents, dreams and in response to divine interventions. When he described the visit of the Queen of Sheba to King Solomon, she is full of wondrous amazement at the king's wisdom, but also at the sacrificial system of the law, and the temple itself.

In the Hebrew Bible wonder was sometimes linked with fear, but such fear marked religious belief, rather than terror. More commonly the experience of wonder linked with expectation of the coming Messiah and hope for future redemption. Hosea 3:5; Micah 7:15; 7:17; 2 Esdras 13:30; Isaiah 52:15 and Zechariah 14:13 are all good examples of this kind of experience. The Book of Wisdom 5:2 is unusual in giving more what we might call a natural history of wonder, where wonder becomes associated with the continuous renewal and refashioning of the universe by God and wisdom. The Book of Enoch (1 Enoch 14:24) describes wonder in relation to experiences of God, but this is related to future hope.

Is wonder in the Gospel accounts a type of fear that opposes faith, or does it underline religious experience? In the Gospel of John wonder normally describes Jesus' opponents, and twice we find the command not to be amazed. John does not link wonder with miracles in the way found in the other Gospels. In Acts, on the other hand, wonder at times is a prelude to belief, as in Acts 8:13 or Acts 13:12, and at other times to disbelief, as in Acts 13:41. Wonder also arises when the Holy Spirit falls on those who believe, as in Acts 2:7, 2:12 and 10:45. Wonder surfaces on eight occasions when the Apostles perform miracles. In some cases the wonderment leads to allegiance, but the disciples are warned against wonder-working for its own sake, for it may lead to the wrong kind of attachments. This comes through particularly clearly in the Book of Revelation, where a wondrous reaction may lead to repentance, as in Revelation 11:11, but it may also lead to idolatrous worship of Satan, portrayed as the beast or dragon as in Revelation 13:3. This is the wonder of those who are deceived. The Epistles also have some references to wonder, in 2 Thessalonians 1:10, for example, wonder is associated with anticipation of the second coming of Christ. James 2:19, on the other hand, describes wonder as the reaction of demons to God.

From the story so far, wonder can arise from forces that are good or evil in these accounts, and lead to faith or disbelief. All cases seem to point to wonder as a reaction to powers beyond the world, rather than wonderment experienced as an outcome of what is perceived to be the norm. Wonder seems to lift those who experience it in these accounts out of self to the point of decision. This corresponds with more contemporary explorations of wonder as that related to what might be termed psychological peak experiences.[5] But it does not prejudge which way an individual will decide.

It is worth looking at Mark in more detail, since of the 32 references to wonder in Mark, 10 are specific to that Gospel, and Matthew's account of wonder is less varied and intense.[6] Mark is interesting, as he seems to associate wonder with obedience in the first half of the Gospel, often associated with acts perceived as the intervention of God. Many of those who come into contact with Jesus find reasons for wonderment both in what he says and in his identity. When Mark describes acts of God that serve to bring in God's reign, for example, physical healings and experiences of forgiveness, then wonder follows. In the second half of the Gospel, wonder arises out of the authority of Jesus' ministry, often associated with the expectation of future restoration at the end times. Whenever and wherever God seems to break in and demonstrate the rule of God, wonderment follows. This authority applies not just over human diseases, but also over the natural world: calming the storm, walking on the water, the accounts of Jesus becoming transfigured on Mount Tabor, and so on. The miracle accounts included in many cases a sense of uncanny energy, bringing those who witnessed them close to a sense of awesome terror. As one might expect, wonder also accompanies the account of Jesus' Passion. Jesus himself also experienced awe in the Garden of Gethsemane in Mark 14:34. Wonder, as one might expect, permeated the climax of the Gospel accounts of the resurrection in 16:1–8. The proof of divine activity even in the Passion comes through the experience of awe and wonder of those who witnessed Jesus' Passion. The wonderment leads to belief and obedience, but only in the case of the disciples. Wonder seems to accompany the Gospel to such an extent that Timothy Dwyer suggests that 'one is left with an impression of the numinous surrounding the entire Gospel of Mark'.[7]

PHILOSOPHY OF WONDER

Mark seems to link wonder with the experience of God as wholly Other, what Rudolf Otto has discussed as consisting of three elements.[8] In the first place there is a feeling of dread, awfulness. In the second place there is an overpowering sense of God's majesty. In the third place there is a sense of energy and urgency, including a sense of vitality. Such a reaction to God as the Holy One might go some way to guard us against the danger of interpreting God as somehow a concrete object of our worship, so that God comes to be viewed as an object alongside other objects.[9]

Wonder experienced as awe affirms the possibility of God acting in the world and opens up a space for the transcendent, without naming what that might be. Wonder on one level may be found in the experiences of nature, in the sense of the enchantment of the natural world with the sacred. This is not so much God as Other, but now God as experienced within the natural world. In this sense it is the opposite to the philosophy of the early writing of Martin Heidegger, where the world is experienced as deprived of religious sentiment, or any notions of God at all, a secularised and disenchanted place. Lash believes that the tension between these two philosophical views of the world, as pagan and secular, that the world is impregnated with the sacred or that the world is deprived of it, amounts to a natural cycle that marks human identity in a particular way.[10] But he also suggests that humanity goes beyond this to consider other possibilities, which he believes find expression in art and culture. I suggest that the very openness to such possibilities includes the experience of wonder, for it seeks to point to the reality of God expressed in concrete ways, so that we discern God as 'like forgiveness and non-violence, solidarity with the victims, the achievement of communion in the one world to which we all belong'.[11] In other words, while with Lash I agree that God is discoverable within the human story, I would suggest, more broadly, that God is also discoverable within the cosmological story as well.

Austin Farrer's book *The Glass of Vision* challenges the idea that God somehow works from 'outside' human experience, and in one sense is similar to Nicholas Lash's insistence that human speech about God necessarily arises from words and images that come from the fabric of the created world.[12] How might we interpret the meaning of supernatural knowledge? For Farrer this means being transposed into the divine centre of activity, so that he can say that a supernatural act is not so much an act *outside* nature, which is the more commonly held definition, as 'the opening of the finite to the infinite'.[13] He also believed that if the finite were to be divinised such that its distinct creaturely nature disappeared, then this would be equivalent to annihilation. Hence, the divinised world has some continuity with the natural world, but experiences a new dimension, one that has its origin in God. As one might anticipate, in Christ the finite and infinite in some sense coincide with each other, so that Christ is the 'coincidence of supernaturalised manhood and self-bestowing deity'.[14] Farrer believes that Christ's message is mediated through images, images of the kingdom of God as God's enthroned majesty, the Son of Man that expresses true humanity, and Israel, as the family of God. These scriptural images are, for Farrer, the true source of revelation, over and above theological speculation about the Gospels. If this is true, then the wonder associated with the coming of the kingdom in Mark discussed above is also primarily about revelation, but it is revelation experienced through a divinised world.

Farrer also has something to say about the scientist's experience of wonder. In the first place, the scientist may experience:

> ... constant amazement at the mysterious nature which the world must be supposed to have in itself, so as to be the sort of world which yields such complex and ordered responses to his yardstick method. But this amazement, this almost religious awe, does not find direct expression in his scientific activity; in so far as he entertains such feelings, he is more of a metaphysician than a pure scientist. That is only another way of saying, that as well as being a scientist he is a man:

and indeed, most scientists are human.[15]

Of course, to suggest that scientists operate by 'measurement' methods that then lead to an experience of awe and wonder tends to dumb down the initial experience of wonderment that first inspired the scientific activity. He seems to be a child of his time in speaking about science in the way he does; theories about general relativity and the uncertainty principle later challenged the Newtonian world. Yet he anticipated a fuller understanding in his argument that the scientist needed to go beyond the 'yardstick' itself and reach for comprehension of the natural world as a profound mystery which needed further exploration. This leads to respect for material being as such, in much the same way as respect for persons is only sustainable by going beyond the tests applied to them in particular ways. He is, in other words, committed to realism, but in a way that is informed by metaphysics, so that 'the metaphysician's method is to keep breaking his yardstick against the requirement of real truth.'[16] One method is to use analogy, but analogies themselves need more and more modification so that they become suited to the mysterious reality that they are being used to describe.

Nature, for Farrer, provides what he calls a 'colour box of analogies', the fact that it is not a clear form of knowledge shows that this is true of all knowledge, not just knowledge about God. He also thinks that we perform acts that in some sense prejudge our subsequent reflection, so that 'By this analogy we might expect that our first thoughts about God must be involuntary too; only when we had begun to think about God could we elaborate and refine at will our mental picture of God.'[17] This may be a helpful way of teasing out what we have already discussed about wonder in the New Testament. Wonder is, in one sense, an involuntary act. But it is only when we have begun to think about what this means that it serves to shape our mental image of what God is like. Such a mental image or analogy is symbolic of the infinite, for the mind 'cannot become aware of the infinite except by symbolising it in terms of the finite'.[18] It is, if you like, a double act whereby the sublime is in itself somewhat ambiguous, hanging 'between earth and heaven'. According to Farrer, the mind is bound to tip in one of two directions, as the two cannot be held in balance. In much the same way wonder may lead to belief in the transcendent, or unbelief. Yet while the transcendent for those early disciples was perceived more like a breaking into the natural order of things, the experience of the Holy that wonder in the natural world invites is more like a discovery of the presence of God in all things, a poetic appreciation of nature as sacrament to God's glory.

A SPIRITUALITY OF WONDER

Wonder as rooted in feelings experienced in the human mind is an unlikely candidate for a systematic treatment of theology. One might expect it to be more suited to more mystical experiences of God, even if that mysticism is nature mysticism, arising out of a sense of the numinous in nature. Yet the theologians of the early church had none of the categories of division that now dominate modern theological discourse.

Contemporary theologians who draw on the theme of wonder are more likely to be found in the Orthodox tradition. Bishop Seraphim Sigrist outlines a theology of wonder that includes a series of reflections on different aspects of daily life as that immersed in wonder. He cites St Isaac of Syria in suggesting that we read the Bible as 'enveloped in Wonder', so that 'integrated knowledge is Wonder in God ... this is the way to come in the freedom of immortal life'.[19]

What themes are of particular significance in a spirituality of wonder? In the first place, as in the case of wisdom, silence acts like a matrix within which the Word is embedded and through which a theology of wonder arises. But this means that silence is not simply the absence of sound, but something more active; some might go as far as saying that it has an autonomous reality. In the Eucharist we pass into a silence that is also an acceptance of our death, a surrender of our lives to God, knowing that God then returns that life. For while our own silence may be full of awareness of what we have lost or our own sense of death, that silence which has its source in God is full of life and light, and the power of Christ's resurrection. One might even say that the silence itself speaks a Word to us in the context of the liturgy and prayer. Such experience is accompanied by wonder, for, as in Mark, it announces the breaking in of the reign of God. With St Isaac of Syria we might say that 'Silence is the Sacrament of the world to come.'[20] Yet such silence also connects with the whole of creation, as the Psalmist recognised when he claimed that 'the heavens declare the glory of God ... No utterance at all, no speech, not a sound to be heard' (Psalm 19:1–3). In this case it was the Wisdom of God made manifest in creation that is the declaration of God's glory; acknowledgement of that wisdom as founded in God leads into an experience of wonder, embedded in silence. In this way, the Eastern tradition celebrates what might be called a cosmic liturgy, so that 'the inner Liturgy of the heart, and the Liturgy of the gathered Church, and the Liturgy of the Universe itself, all reflect each other, and, each inseparable from the others, they form finally a single Liturgy.'[21]

What of pilgrimage? How do the wonders recounted by those stories of the search for the Holy Grail bear on the theme of a journey into wonder? While it is possible for stories about wonder to lack depth, or that sense of the numinous, there are others that seem to be more charged with wonder in the theological sense of the term. Stories about the Holy Grail are those stories about how the chalice of the Last Supper is entrusted to Joseph of Arimathea, who brought it to the Western world. The knights of King Arthur are charged with the quest for the Grail at a Pentecost gathering, but only Galahad, Perceval and Bors achieve the quest. The medieval stories about the search are a reaction to the more formalised rationalistic definitions of the Eucharist in the Latin Church. It is useful to look beyond these stories and see what the Grail signifies, namely the presence of Christ in the world, so that Sergii Bulgakov claims that:

> The Holy Grail (that is how we will conditionally call the blood and water that came out of Christ's side) is not offered for communion, but abides in the world, as the

mysterious holiness of the world, as the power of life, as the fire in which the world will be transfigured into a new heaven and a new earth.[22]

Teresa of Cartegena (b. *c*.1415–20) was a medieval mystic who devoted one of her major works to the theme of wonder.[23] Her first major work, *Grove of the Infirm*, was a reflection on her experience of deafness. Many women at the time experienced anxiety about authorship; a common view doubted that women could write at all. She wrote *Wonder at the Works of God* in response to these criticisms. She is particularly scathing of the kind of wonder expressed by those who doubted her authenticity, in other words, those who believed that a man had written in her place. For her there are two types of wonder: there is wonder mixed with devotion and faith which praises and venerates God, through marvelling in the gifts of God's blessing, but then there is a wonder mixed with incredulity that is offensive to God because more importance is given to the phenomenon that inspires wonder than to the divine source. In other words, wonder can lead towards spiritual growth, or its opposite. She also helpfully names two kinds of blessings. First, there are the blessings of nature or good fortune that may lead to particular virtues such as bravery or understanding. Second, there are the blessings of grace, which are more extraordinary.

She also wanted to affirm that we should see all things in the created world as being charged with wonder:

> ... so that the least thing that this Sovereign and most powerful Creator has made is no less wonderful than the greatest. This is because the smallest thing in the world, like the greatest, could not be found unless God's omnipotence created it. And if all things, great and small, created by God's omnipotence are marvellous and worthy of great Wonder and he can make on earth and in heaven whatever he pleases, why do we marvel at some things more than others?[24]

She followed Augustine in his suggestion that the way the 5000 were governed was just as marvellous as the satisfaction of their hunger through the miracle of the loaves and fishes. In other words, we need to begin to see the works of God as evidenced throughout our daily life, not just in the unusual or the spectacular experiences. In this way 'those we see occur daily in the natural course of things are no less marvellous or worthy of admiration than those that happen rarely or at great intervals of time.'[25] In much the same way she argued that just as God is free to give gifts where God chooses, so it is no greater wonder to find that a woman can write, however unusual that might seem to her opponents!

The prime motivation for her writing a book on wonder was to turn around that very wonder that she found offensive in her opponents and to find theological support for wonder as that which permeates the creation. It therefore forms a narrative of the way wonder can be used or misused. She did, nonetheless, seem to accept a stereotypical view of women as fearful and faint-hearted, seemingly 'protected' by powerful men. At the same time, her analogy of gender differences with plant and tree life, naming women as like the inner core and men as the outer bark, offers another view of women at the time, for while what may seem fragile is the inner core, it is also, she suggests, that which is the most life-giving, compared to the dead exterior that merely offers protection! The complementary nature of men and women was, for her, a source of profound wonder 'ordered by God's great wisdom'.[26] The difference between the sexes, she concludes, is not so much based on degrees of excellence, but for the purposes of preserving human nature. Contemporary feminist theories of difference would say no less, though they would be less comfortable with the idea that women need the protection of men.

She also argues that we need to move our wonder from the things of the world to God, even starting with contemplation of God first in order to wonder aright,[27] so that:

> ... to marvel at God's wondrous works with devotion and sound spirit, we should first elevate our wonder to the

omnipotence, wisdom and goodness of our most excellent
Father, and then lower our understanding to marvel at the
blessings and benefits, mercy and grace that he grants to
human creatures. (p.95)

Yet she finds that the first kinds of blessings that we might
experience come from divine providence, blessings of nature or
fortune that are experienced as gift. In this way she suggests:

And first we should marvel at our general blessings, blessings of nature and blessings of fortune, which are very great
and marvellous. And without doubt we will find in them
enough to sustain our wonder for a long time, and after this
we will marvel even more at the exceptional or special
blessings that are called blessings of grace. And whence
comes grace if not from God? (p.95)

In other words, the special blessings experienced as the work of
God's grace take us even further on the journey into wonder. In
addition, if others have received special gifts, then the focus of
our wonder should not be on them, but on God, who gives these
blessings. Moreover, if we direct our wonder at God, then we will
give praise where it is due, to God, rather than to mortals. A
suitably focused experience of wonder will allow our awe to
'travel a straight path, for we shall venerate and honor the things
He created and their Sovereign Maker' (p.97).

Cartegena has given us a tapestry of how to wonder, yet she
also recognised that finding wonder in God is coincident with
discovering God's Wisdom. For through the work of God's
Wisdom humanity becomes wise. In this way she can pray,
'Come, send my Lord, the wisdom at the seat of Your marvellous
greatness, so that it may be with me and mould me, and I may
know always what is acceptable before You.'[28] Yet the mood
expressed in the wonder of God for Cartegena seems to be at
God's characteristics as all-powerful and all-wise. The theme of
beauty does not come over; rather, she pays particular attention
to the idea of gift – that all life and all blessings are from God,

and so enriching our sense of wonder. In a more general sense the spiritual journey is one that is about paying attention, and the ability to wonder presupposes that ability.[29] Cartegena knew what it was to pay attention to God in silence and reflection and so became aware of the deeper mystery of all of life as a gift, beckoning us towards the giver of that gift. Wonder also accompanies us if we make that journey.

BEAUTY AND WONDER IN GOD

In the eighteenth century, philosophers made a distinction between beauty and the sublime, so beauty became associated with the decorative, pleasant or pretty. This is not the meaning of beauty we are concerned with here. Beauty, rather, can become the source of feelings of wonder, and beauty associated with the sublime is the kind of theological wonder that we have been discussing. Beauty is important as it shows that God's glory as revealed to us is not just about holiness, righteousness and power, but, more important, something communicable and intrinsically delightful.[30] In this way glory calls forth not just awe and penitence, but also deep rejoicing.

Beauty in the classical tradition was associated with goodness and truth, not isolated in aesthetic detachment from moral elements in the way it seems to be today. Beauty that is divine, according to Gregory of Nyssa, inflames our desire for God; it is like a 'stretching out towards an ever greater embrace of divine glory'.[31] In addition, beauty seems to cross boundaries that we somewhat artificially set up between supernatural and natural, nature and grace. In other words, beauty shows that created nature is itself full of divine splendour.

St Bonaventure believed in an analogy between the beauty that we experience in this world and divine beauty. According to his view, the Word is not so much the idea that overshadows particular expressions of creation, but the infinite rhetoric that enables divine speech to become articulated in particular ways. The analogy of beauty between God and the world allows us to think of creation as free expressions of love and delight, praising the

Creator even through its variety and immensity.[32] Does the ascent from the creation to the Creator take sufficient account of suffering? He would have certainly been unaware of the extent of this compared with current knowledge, but beauty does not necessarily mean absence from pain for, according to the theologian Hans urs von Balthasar, beauty is also present in the Crucified One, just as wonder is present here, so beauty also accompanies this wonder. The danger that Bonaventure seeks to correct, and one that is equally prevalent today, is to see the world as self-directed autonomy, existing apart from God and in isolation from God's grace. In addition, analogy means that we preserve the particularities of individual creatures; they are not simply annihilated through sublimation into the divine silence. This means that perfection is achieved not by imposing an order of correspondence, but through ever more elaborate expressions of complexity.

In the contemporary world of physics the experience of wonder is also associated with a search for beauty, which in its turn is seen as a guide to truth.[33] Paul Davies acknowledges the role of beauty in guiding scientists in their speculative physics. He asks why beauty is apparent in fundamental theoretical physics if it is, according to the evolutionary paradigm, entirely biologically programmed. He believes that one can only explain the presence of beauty in physics if it is more than biology at work, so that human aesthetic appreciation stems from something more pervasive than biology reflected in the fundamental laws of physics. In this way, wonder and beauty are companions of each other, reaching towards the same goal, namely a discovery of God as the author of that beauty.

Yet there is a difference between the kind of beauty that the physicists speak about and the beauty of the classic Christian tradition. For in the latter beauty arises out of the experience of goodness, and resides in a particular way in the person of Christ. The beauty of Christ points not just to the affirmation of the order of the world, as described by Paul Davies and others, or its annihilation in an eschatology of secular physics, but rather its transfiguration.[34] Just as philosophy in Aquinas' time could only take us so far and point merely towards the bare existence of God, so the divine essence remains beyond the grasp of science. It is a mistake, then, to think that Aquinas thought that signs in the natural world are sufficient grounds for belief. It is also a mistake to think that the signs dimly seen in the natural world are in some sense apart from divine revelation. Thomas believed, unlike Aristotle, that speculative science fails to satisfy fully the human desire to know. At the same time he acknowledges an ordering of goods, so that the highest good does not, as in Plato, deny the validity of the limited goods found in the created world.

We arrive at this point at a discussion of the way grace works in the world, perfecting and elevating human nature, rather than destroying it. Aristotelian philosophy acknowledged that there is a goal that escapes its grasp. Thomas believed that this goal is the transcendent, but qualified this by suggesting that a complete vision of God is impossible in this life. But such vision is always grounded in the concrete and particular story of Jesus, so resisting the tendency for abstraction. In speaking of the contemplative life in the third part of his major theological treatise, the *Summa Theologiae*, Aquinas believed that love of God enabled the beauty of the divine to become evident, and the perception of beauty also stirs up desire and love for God. In this way we can think of beauty as that which encircles the contemplative life.[35]

What is beauty according to Aquinas?[36] For him, it includes clarity, meaning not just in the material world, but also in the intellectual and spiritual worlds as well. It also embraces the idea of proportion, or what is needed for a particular purpose or end. Thirdly, beauty means integrity, or completion; it is a realisation of the perfection of something. These three marks of the beautiful also apply to the second person of the Trinity, so that beauty is rooted not just in abstract speculation, but also in Christ's personhood. Grace acts by restoring the good to the realm of beauty. But if beauty is also about perception, then it is linked not just with wonder, but with wisdom also. Aquinas draws an analogy between the work of creation and God acting as master artist, again implying that creation is not just good, but also beautiful. But the differences in this analogy are important. For

[147]

example, God makes out of freedom and through the bestowal of being, rather than simply by introducing form into pre-existing matter.

How does wisdom relate to beauty? Like the fourth-century father, Gregory of Nyssa, St Symeon the New Theologian, writing at the turn of the tenth century, was happy to see in the beauty of creation a form of 'symphony' of praise to God as Creator, pointing also to divine Wisdom.[37] In one of St Symeon's hymns we find the doxological dimension to the created world, thus:

> O the depths of riches and divine knowledge,
> O the depth of Your wisdom, my God, all bountiful!
> That from the greatness and beauty of created things
> You might learn of the incomprehensible Wisdom
> of God.[38]

Sergei Bulgakov connects beauty discovered in creation with the active working of the Holy Spirit.[39] He asserts that the glory of creation is a reflection of the conferral of divine Glory, which in its innermost self also expresses beauty through trinitarian inner transparency one to another. Hence beauty, like wisdom, is found in all three persons of the Trinity, originating primarily in the Father. Bulgakov is preoccupied with the source of beauty in the divine life, rather than the more Aristotelian movement of beauty from the experience of the world that we find in Aquinas. Yet he is perhaps more aware of the seductive dangers of beauty, that it can serve to draw attention away from God by becoming the object of human possession. This also means that the beauty of creation is arrested by the dark shadow that exists in creaturely wisdom. There is a sense in which creation is waiting in anticipation for the spiritual transformation towards wisdom and beauty that will only happen at the second coming of Christ.

Hans urs von Balthasar is also aware of the dangers of beauty in the human realm, but he more specifically places Christ as an icon of beauty as that which challenges all other forms of beauty. In some way this is analogous to the Wisdom of the cross, except now it is the beauty of the cross that challenges human appreciation of beauty.[40] The beauty of Christ, like the Wisdom of the cross, is a hidden beauty, so that,

> As the incarnate art of God (ars divina), he is the appearing of absolute beauty, and this appearing is free from all outward show, for it is in itself the substantial truth.[41]

How might we think of the difference between beauty and wisdom, if both are associated with the perfection anticipated in the journey towards wonder? Perhaps this difference is best anticipated by looking to more practical aspects of the Christian life. Prudence, or practical wisdom, has to do with discernment and correct decision-making. Temperance, on the other hand, is more about not grasping more for myself than I really need. In as much as it is about knowing what is seemly and in right proportion it is related to beauty. But just as prudence is a prelude to true development of temperance, for it allows correct discernment of what this means, so wisdom is a prelude to beauty, even if beauty arises out of its flowering. The experience of both wisdom and beauty can lead to a sense of wonder, and wonder is also present even when the theological root of that wisdom and beauty is severed from view.

CONCLUSIONS

The philosopher Ludwig Wittgenstein echoed the sentiment of many philosophers when he claimed that 'the wonderful thing is that the world exists. That there is what there is.'[42] So far we have acknowledged the natural emotion of wonder and seen how it is also bound up with religious experience. In the world of early Greek and Roman literature, the experience of wonder was associated with invention by gods or God. But wonder itself may not lead to religious faith; in John's Gospel, for example, wonder is more like incredulity, a reaction of Jesus' opponents. Wonder in Acts is more mixed, sometimes belief follows the experience of wonder, and sometimes it does not. In Mark wonder is much more positive, pervading the accounts of special healings, acts of reconciliation, and marking the authority of Jesus over the natural elements. For Mark, wonder is indicative of the coming of the reign of God. The experience of wonder marks out a more general sense of enchantment with the world, in opposition to those who no longer experienced the world as having a numinous or a sacred dimension. The movement of humanity beyond these two alternatives becomes possible through acknowledging the presence of God in human history and the history of the cosmos, in much the same way that Mark highlights the presence of wonder in specific acts that mark the presence of the kingdom of God.

Does this necessarily entail a vision of a God who simply intervenes in human and cosmic history? I suggest this is not so, for we can think of the experience of God as being more akin to the openness of the finite to the infinite. Wonder is in one sense an involuntary act, but deeper reflection on its meaning requires more thought. The Eastern Orthodox theological tradition keeps the mystical and more systematic together, which is why there is a place here for a theology of wonder. In fact, Orthodoxy's emphasis on the resurrection means that wonder finds its place not just in the Divine Liturgy, but also in reflections on eternal life. The search for the Holy Grail in the Western church is a journey into wonder, a reaction to the more sterile formulas of the time. While some of such accounts are fanciful, theistic wonder breaks through. Teresa of Cartagena offered us a helpful guide into two kinds of wonder, the wonder that comes from disbelief, and the wonder that is properly rooted in faith and experience of God. The natural world can, in faith, promote our praise of the Creator. Yet the experience of grace also takes us deeper on the journey into wonder.

In what sense might contemplation also include the idea of beauty? Certainly, for physicists, beauty does not have the more shallow meaning associated with simply being pretty or attractive, but is about alliance with truth. Yet in the classical tradition, beauty and truth were also joined with goodness, and while beauty was more cognitive, goodness reflected our will. The grace of God transforms goodness so that it also becomes beautiful. Just as the Wisdom of God is also represented in the

Crucified One, so, paradoxically, Christ is named as the one who expresses perfect beauty. Beauty is about completion and perfection, and the work of the Holy Spirit points towards this perfection in the natural world. The experience of beauty through wisdom marks its completion, even though we can acknowledge with Aquinas that we never finally arrive at a complete vision of God, the beatific vision, in this life. In this sense the journey into wonder is like the search for wisdom – also a journey that is always on the way, never complete.

EIGHT

WEAVING WONDER AND WISDOM

So far we have taken a journey that has moved from wonder to wisdom and back to wonder again. But how might we gather up these threads in order to give a sense of integrated knowledge which wisdom speaks about? If wisdom is about density of meaning in different scriptural interpretations,[1] as surely it is, so, then, wisdom also aims to present a picture of the whole that enlightens rather than fragments knowledge from disparate sources. This chapter will attempt to offer such an integration of the key ideas presented in this book in an attempt to weave wonder and wisdom together. For it is through wonder and wisdom that a deeper spirituality can surface which serves to awaken an integrated knowledge in theology and science, without skating over the tensions between them. If wisdom is the voice for theology at the boundary of science, so wonder reminds theology that science too offers its own wisdom that needs to be taken into account. If wonder is common to both scientific discovery and religious experience, wisdom offers a way of distinguishing where that wondering leads away from the truth. If truth is only ever a dim reflection in a mirror, then wonder at the Wisdom of God points to a future hope where perfected knowledge becomes possible. Above all, both wonder and wisdom are accompanied by love, Love of God for creation, love of humanity for God interwoven with love of humanity for the universe and life in all its rich diversity and plenitude.

In the first place, we can go back to the question I asked at the beginning of this book. Does wonder arise out of a sense of instability and at the edge of the known, or does it arise from a sense of order or perfection in the natural world? The answer must surely be both. Paradoxically both are appropriate forms of wonder, for both may lead to a profound sense of the sublime, that biologists speak about when they describe curious observations as 'uncanny'. Perhaps, also, contemporary biologists and physicists are less cagey about using the term wonder to describe what they have discovered. While all scientific discoveries are open to revision, they are also experienced as the real, in the sense of an encounter with reality. The fact that there is anything at all in the universe is a source for profound wonder for most cosmologists. In this way wonder and curiosity are now reunited after a lengthy divorce, even though traces of disdain for wonder may creep in through associating it with scientific books designed for children. For if wonder is simply about childhood, then this implies a lack of rationality and a lack of depth of understanding, a naive approach that might be expressed as either enthusiasm in science or superstition in religion. Yet there is also a positive sense in which childhood wonder is entirely appropriate. For a child is not encumbered to the same extent with presuppositions arising from habitual scepticism about the possibility of the new and different emerging. Even Christ speaks of the need to become as little children in order to enter into the kingdom of God. This does not mean a superstitious acceptance without reason, but a willingness to be open to the possibility of finding the truth in unexpected places.

What then of wisdom? Wisdom is now becoming more fashionable in theological circles, so much so that David Ford can even suggest that 'I am conceiving Christian theology as a seeking of wisdom.'[2] But in what sense might this claim be true? Certainly wisdom in a philosophical sense means reflection on life, rather than simply knowledge, and it is true that theology is also concerned with life experiences as well. The way of wisdom in the Hebrew Bible was one learnt in the family or through education, building up particular traits of character, but rooted in the fear of the Lord as the beginning of wisdom (Proverbs 9:10). Human wisdom, also, comes through habitual patterns of behaviour that some neuroscientists believe could change the way our brains are networked together. We become, quite literally, transformed through the renewal of our minds.

Yet the Hebrew tradition also speaks of wisdom in terms that imply close attention to detail, a paying attention, which then indirectly leads to wisdom. If wisdom becomes the object of obsession, then it is sure to pass us by, for wisdom comes, as it were, secretly in its own way. There is a paradox here. For on the one hand, we are encouraged to seek wisdom and desire her over all material goods. But on the other hand, too much straining after wisdom can itself become a source of vanity, a seeking after wind, as Qoheleth reminds us. One of the ways in which we can avoid the danger of self-centredness is by paying attention to the created order, which the Psalmists also encouraged, in their own way. Here wonder and wisdom are hand in hand. What kind of wisdom emerges from looking at the wonder of the universe? Our knowledge now is more profound than that of those early writers, and an occasion for even greater wonder. Twelve or fifteen billion years ago the universe came into existence through the Big Bang, the theory most in favour at present. Even the ancients speculated about such an origin, but they did not have the tools to test alternatives.

We now know that mysterious dark matter makes up the bulk of the universe, and the most wondrous aspect is that there is something rather than nothing. The matter of the universe is like the left-over fragments of a massive creation of space and time itself evolving from the Singularity out of forms that escape definition in terms of physical reality. Gravitational and repulsive forces act in concert like a dance for the emerging universe, generating enough order while allowing the free play of contingency. The physical laws of the universe seem to be fine-tuned in order to allow the formation of the earth and the possibility of life on the planet. Scientists too, attempt to imitate these initial conditions in order to simulate that early primordial soup. Such experiments are at the border of our unknowing, having common ground with explorations into space, cosmologists now wishing to cross boundaries even beyond our solar system. Such searches have much in common with those early medievalists who believed that at the outer limits of the known world there were wondrous regions of mystery, waiting to be discovered. Is there life on other planets in our universe? Certainly, calculations of the possible physical conditions needed suggest that this would not be impossible. Yet life first began on earth some 4 billion years ago, while a mere 4 million years ago our earliest hominid ancestors appeared, with our own species, *Homo sapiens*, appearing a paltry 250,000 years or so ago.

Is our cosmos a harbinger of deep promise, as some contemporary theologians have suggested? Physicists argue otherwise, that in the far-flung future life will no longer be possible, the universe will have dissipated its energy, ending in terms reminiscent of apocalyptic predictions of the ancient prophets. We are left with a dilemma. On the one hand, physics and cosmology are witness to a profound ordering in the universe, which seems to permit life to exist and demonstrates an ordering even apparently 'designed' for such life. But on the other hand, the final destination seems to be futile, ending in catastrophic terms, with little possibility of a reprieve. What are we to make of such paradox? My suggestion is that the wisdom of science on its own fails at this point, for science may make predictions, but it is not prophetic. The prophetic tradition sees calamity and predictions of calamity as ways of speaking about the kingdom of God. Mortality itself may seem less threatening than this ultimate collapse. Yet the Christian message also speaks to our human mortal condition, promising that this life and all its diversity is not the final word. Hope in the resurrection is a counter-cultural hope that points beyond itself to new beginnings, perhaps a different order of space and time that have not yet been identified by contemporary physical science.[3] Certainly, Jesus' resurrection appearances suggested as much – he was able to pass through walls, but he was also capable of eating and drinking. However sceptical we might be tempted to be about the literalness or otherwise of these accounts, they demonstrate that the resurrection life is not the same as life on earth, but it has some continuity with it.

We are, by nature, naturally attracted to life in all its diversity, we have what E. O. Wilson describes as *biophilia*. Such biophilia can lead those scientists with no professed religious sense, including Richard Dawkins, who is openly hostile to religion, to speak of wonder in the natural world. Yet finding wonder through natural history has a long tradition, beginning with the early Celtic saints, evident in the works of St Francis of Assisi and other spiritual writers such as Bonaventure, and culminating in the more recent tradition of being both priest and naturalist. John Ray began a tradition of also being fascinated by the scientific elements of his botanical study; he saw no incompatibility with his religious faith. If anything, he saw it as a religious duty to search after the details of the creation in order to discover the mirror of God's appearing. The choice that Annie Dillard presents us with, of viewing the natural processes in life as either the result of random contingency or an intimate involvement of the Creator in each and every biological process, seems unnecessarily stark. For there are other ways of being a scientist, which allow an integration of scientific investigation with a profound sense of the unity and mystery of the natural order. In other words, a religious sensibility hovering under the surface, as in the more personal reflections of that great geneticist Barbara McClintock. Pierre Teilhard de Chardin spoke of no less in his great vision of the universe as the divine milieu in which God is actively present, though allowing the world to be itself.

Indeed, if wisdom is about living in unity with the way things are, as some evolutionary biologists have suggested, then wisdom is also open to the possibility that there are sources of knowledge that point beyond materialism. Evolution itself seems to be limited to certain paths, restrained in particular ways, rather than the outcome of a purely random drunken walk towards higher complexity. If this is the case, then this brings back once more the question that surfaces in contemporary physics, namely, is God also a designer, who has designed evolution for a particular purpose? The notion of God as a designer proved problematic for those early natural theologians following John Ray, who wanted to see the wisdom of God in all the works of creation. For once natural selection offered a biological explanation for diversity and patterns in evolution, so the idea of a designer no longer seemed necessary. In other words, it just seemed like a design, but in reality it was the result of natural selection. The metaphor of God as designer is unhelpful in the sense that it implies fixity of outcome for evolution though, in as much as evolution is under constraints, one might add that it is not entirely random either. It is more helpful, perhaps, to see in the natural world those intimations of the sacred that then pave the way for more profound searching and religious belief. Then, in the light of renewed faith, God could once more be claimed as the author of that creative process.

The notion of design is also problematic in another way, for it implies that suffering is built into the order of nature in a deliberate way. Suffering then becomes the principle of creation; nature takes on a cruciform shape that makes suffering inevitable. But such a notion would imply that God deliberately set out to punish the natural world through suffering, even prior to the appearance of humanity. Amoral suffering was the experience of millions upon millions of species through extinction, even before that first fatal deliberate turning away from God by humankind told in the story of the Fall of humanity. What are we to make of this kind of profound suffering? Certainly, it cannot simply be connected with human sin or even the human capacity for freedom in the way that some theologians have tended to assume. A theological response would seek less to explain such suffering away, as to show how God has acted in the light of such suffering. The tradition of God being present with those who suffer through the *Shekinah*, or presence of the Spirit, comes to a climax in the suffering of Christ on the cross. Yet this suffering is not about God punishing the Son in our place. This doctrine of the atonement makes God out to be a monster, a Father torturing his Son. Rather, such suffering came through the love of God for all creation and the desire of God for reconciliation with all things through vulnerable giving up of power and identification with our human, frail and mortal condition.

That great hymn to the Colossians in the first chapter speaks not just about the reconciliation possible through the life of the church, but also the cosmic work of Christ as Wisdom, one who is with creation from the beginning of time. Creation and redemption are mysteriously held together. Such Wisdom does not leave creation to its suffering in isolation from God, but mysteriously takes up such pain into the Godhead. It permits a transformation of persons, so that instead of putting humanity first, in what the Russian Orthodox theologian Sergii Bulgakov called *mangodhood*, now humanity becomes capable of *Godmanhood*.[4] Yet the transformation reaches out towards creation itself, so that it too becomes caught up in the transforming work of Christ. Such transformation is not visible here on earth except through the agency of humanity acting on behalf of creation. Bulgakov believed that we must work for the resurrection of nature, to endow it with the life and meaning it once had in Eden.[5] Yet his suggestion of a return to Eden may not take sufficient account of the creativity that still exists in creation, for it implies a fixity and perfection of form in the beginning. The Colossian hymn also points to humanity as the place where human sinfulness becomes transformed, and this has a ripple effect on the rest of the created order, pointing to its future redemption. Richard Bauckham concludes that the great hymn to wisdom in the letter to the Colossians is not so much about anthropocentric superiority, as showing humanity its place and role as healer of creation. Hence:

> That recognition of chaos and evil at the heart of human history requires us to relate to the rest of God's creation in humility and trust, with love rather than with mastery, in search of the peace that is the well-being of all creatures, not the well-being of ourselves at the expense of all others. That is one of the paths along which wisdom is to be found.[6]

The mystery of why such suffering is present is still there, but human agency, working in imitation of Christ, can seek to identify with that suffering and, where possible, ameliorate it for the well-being of creatures other than humankind. Such gestures of human kindness towards animals and towards other creatures become signs of the reign of God, intimations of that future life where God will be all in all. How far humankind can also work to improve on nature through creative intervention, such as that in genetic science, remains a question that requires practical wisdom.[7] Above all, crucified wisdom invites humanity to turn away from arrogant claims for self-aggrandisement, and learn to walk humbly with God and all of God's creatures. Just as Christ emptied himself of power by identification with human frailty, so humanity needs to let go of those forms of power that dominate others.

In what sense is wisdom also feminine wisdom? Certainly, identification with frailty does not mean a lack of self-assertiveness where the occasion arises or permits. Rather, wisdom is about knowing what is appropriate to given circumstances. Such wisdom speaks of practical wisdom or prudence, a way of taking counsel, judging and acting in a certain way. Human wisdom is patterned after the cross in that it is not just about human self-development in psychological terms, but about being willing to love and perceive what is required for the benefit of the whole community, beyond the demands of family and kin. Such integrated knowledge implies human responsibility, moral integrity and accountability to God and others. Such complex knowledge implies more than a simple passing on of given traits either through memes or through genetic information.

If we seek to explain culture in terms of meme theory two problems arise. In the first place, there needs to be a biological explanation of where memes come from, which seems to be lacking. In the second place, memes imply that cultural ideas are passed on rather like objects from one generation to the next. In practice, human life is far more complex than this might suggest, and wisdom also has the capacity to critique such cultural representations of reality arising out of scientific theory. Humanity makes culture through active projects, rather than through passive acceptance of ideas. Yet in as much as human wisdom is connected with natural wisdom, so there is continuity. Natural wisdom is about the particular way of behaving in tune with the natural environment. It should come as no surprise if some implicit forms of wisdom are found in other species, even unrelated species such as dolphins. Yet the content of that wisdom will be related to survival needs in a way that is very different from the content characteristic of the human community. This need not imply superiority on the part of humans; rather, humanity is geared to specific forms of life that are characteristic of its species. Such forms of life include lifestyle patterns, such as celibacy, that would seem to work against evolutionary advantage. Explaining such behaviour in terms of group esteem and indirect adaptive advantage seems rather wooden.

A characteristic of human wisdom that takes up natural wisdom in a way that is highly distinctive for humans is the perception of God as Wisdom. The content of what that wisdom entails has come through a long search for wisdom through centuries of Judaeo-Christian reflection. Lady Wisdom in the Hebrew Bible is a personification of an aspect of the divine nature. While the starting point for Christian reflection is to see Jesus Christ as the Wisdom of God, this also points to wisdom as a feature of the Godhead in trinitarian terms. Yet we need to be careful here. For God is not envisaged as an object, alongside other objects, in the manner of scientific research. Seeking wisdom is as much about entering into the mystery of who God is in a manner that admits the truth of how little we know or understand about God, that God is not finite and not like human wisdom. Yet wisdom is also positive in that divine Wisdom is characteristic of God even before the creation of the world.

There are two facets to this. On the one hand divine Wisdom is there, ever present in the Trinity, in a way that comes to free expression in the creation of the wonderful universe and wonderful life which humanity inhabits. Such an act of creativity on the part of God is not so much necessary, as an outflowing of divine Love. In one sense we can say that the wisdom of creation mirrors the Wisdom of God. The classical writers spoke of this in terms of natural law, natural law being a participation in the Eternal Law, which is named as Wisdom. Yet this presents us with a 'top down' picture of the activity of God that is only half the story. The other, equally important, aspect is one where wisdom is emerging from the natural order in and through itself; in this way God acquires wisdom from the world that God has made. Such acquisition of wisdom comes to its fullest expression in the person of Jesus Christ. It is in this sense that we can speak of humanity being taken up into God.

Yet we can also go further than this and say that creaturely wisdom is taken up into God as well, through participation. This double movement prevents the ideal of the Wisdom of God becoming a rigid formula into which natural creation must inevitably conform. While there is much strength in Bulgakov's understanding of God as Wisdom in all persons of the Trinity, the movement tends to be portrayed as one-sided, Wisdom from above, God imposing Wisdom on the created order. The other half of the movement, one that is rooted in the everyday and ordinary createdness of things, is one that feminist theologians have highlighted to good effect. Does this mean that divine Wisdom is changed or added to in some way through the natural wisdom? The idea of change is related to mortality, finitude and the space–time continuum in which human life is situated. In God there is no sense of such change; God is immortal and infinite, so it is incorrect to speak of a specific change in God, for God's infinite wisdom is beyond our widest imaginings. This view contrasts with process theology, where God's contingent nature is somehow enriched by creation which serves to contribute directly to who God is.

We are left with an antinomy: two contradictory statements about God that are equally true. On the one hand God did not need to create the world in an absolute sense in order to expand God's Wisdom or God's Love. But on the other hand, it is in the nature of God to love, to exist in relationships, and to be creative. Creativity is expressed through wisdom, so that wisdom in the guise of the Spirit is hovering at the boundary of order and chaos from the beginning, the boundary where new life and new possibilities come into existence. An aspect of this creativity is to let creation be, to show itself forth in natural wisdom that is at once a mirror of divine Wisdom, but also one that offers delight to God; one might even suggest that God wonders at the wisdom of the world God has made. There is an element of surprise that brings joy. The joy of the creature and the joy of the Creator come through one fully participating in the other, so that the wonder of the kingdom of God is as much about premonitions of this future participation in glory.

I have argued throughout this book that both wonder and wisdom involve an attitude that is the opposite of mastery. Both include the sense of openness to the natural world and openness to God. Indeed, it is through wonder that the transcendent energy of being comes into view in the natural world. Yet such hints at the divine presence in all things only really makes sense from the standpoint of faith. The wonder in the world may open up the possibility for religious belief, but it does not tell us what that belief needs to entail. It may even lead down false avenues on its own, for it is undisciplined by wisdom. Our journey into wonder takes us to a threshold, where it is possible to decide for or against religious interpretation of events. Wonder is about being open to the possibility of letting go of previously held views, but it is also vulnerable in that it can veer one way or the other away from the truth that includes goodness and beauty. That truth is always dimly perceived, a cloudy vision of God's Word that is also connected with the search for wisdom.

Given that wonder and wisdom draw on the profound use of the imagination, expressing a resistance to mastery in terms of control, I hinted in the Introduction that a spirituality that draws on wonder and wisdom would appeal to those outside established religious traditions as well as those within. I suggest, in particular, that a spirituality that draws on wonder and wisdom of the natural world as experienced through close observation is one that is in tune with the popular drift towards perceiving nature as sacred. It picks up on the dim perception among many in the Western world that contemporary attitudes to nature and technology have a religious quality to them, in a way that is particularly formative of contemporary cultural history as we know it at present.[8]

Bronislaw Szerszynski argues that there is a general retreat or fragmentation of organised religion in Western societies, but this then leaves not so much a 'secular wasteland, devoid of sacred meaning, but rather ... a huge diversity of forms of enchantment'.[9] There are, in other words, rich profusions of the sacred, bridging the technological and natural worlds, though they are not simply a return to pre-Christian beliefs, for they still echo something of the 'long arc' of the monotheism that once dominated society. I suggest that institutional religion, if it is to survive at all, needs to take into account this cultural trend towards finding the sacred in the natural world, while recognising that the earlier dominant history of monotheism has still left its imprint on the cultural landscape. I believe that such forms of implicit religion are insufficient from a theological point of view, in that while they can open up the conversation, they need to become filled out with particular meanings that draw more fully on classical under-standings of Christian theology. Finding wonder and seeking wisdom might be one way in which more institutional forms of religion can begin to make sense in such a context.

Where might we find everyday examples of how to weave wonder and wisdom in the context of both the institutional church, and those who are somewhat disaffected, at the margins of the church community? Perhaps a good place to start in the institutional church is in the Liturgy, which finds fullest expres-sion in the Holy Eucharist. The start of the Liturgy is the Gloria, an attestation of the wonder of God's creative presence in the world. Here wisdom is present as the Wisdom of the Crucified One. It is also human wisdom, the wisdom of community and family life, the daily task of seeking to unite our life with that of God. In the offering of bread and wine we offer up creation to be blessed and transformed by God's grace. Human wisdom takes us so far, but in order to express the wisdom that comes from God we need the presence of the Holy Spirit with us on our journey. Such a journey into the death and resurrection of Christ, a retelling of the story of the Passion of our Lord, is one that is filled with wonder. This wonder is that which Augustine spoke about, as it is wonder that is dependent on faith, rather than prior to it. Wonder that is faith-filled accompanies the silence of prayer; it is a way of paying attention to God which is more profound than simply listening to the Word alone. Seeking wisdom makes it clear that even the Scriptures have variegated meanings that do not give absolute definitions of what wisdom might be. Yet we can slowly perceive that, by starting with the Love of God expressed in the Crucified One, our own search is likely to be surprised by God's own intentions, for God's Wisdom is always greater than human wisdom.

The searches in science, which may include those who are at the margins of institutional religion, are in one sense analogous to this profoundly religious experience, but also very different. Wonder may accompany that first question at the beginning of a search into the myriad complexities of the universe, or life itself. Wisdom too, is needed in order to uncover more what that wonder means, where it is leading, and how it is opening up a new path to discovery. A scientist also needs to have the humility to let go of previous conceptions of truth; one might even say it is a dim reflection of carrying the cross. Yet the search for wisdom also leads to a deeper form of wonder, one that is filled with a particular kind of knowing. Where wisdom is truncated into simple understanding or acquiring information, wonder seems less likely. Instead, wonder is also present where the boundaries are incomplete, where it becomes impossible to say with absolute certainty what the truth entails. Such is the order of things according to modern physics. Yet the human spirit seems to need to journey into wonder and seek after wisdom, and scientific investigations will fulfil that desire to some extent. Yet true wisdom will not be content with knowledge arising from one slice of reality through science. A scientist who is also a religious believer will give that wonder and wisdom back to God as the source of all wisdom and fountain of all wonder. They will see the material world as permeated with the presence of God's Spirit, and will sense the numinous in all things. Such awareness can expand our understanding of who God is, for the God of history is also the Lord of creation.

The resurrection appearances of Christ all have a common thread, often a failure by the disciples to fully recognise who he was. Yet there was something different about him that clouded their perception. The continuity remained, for it was through his actions or words or gestures that they came to see the truth. In much the same way, there will always remain an element of mystery hovering over the search for wisdom, otherwise that search would be complete. Such completion is impossible in this life, which is why prose fails to express the weaving of wonder and wisdom adequately. I will therefore conclude with a poem by Gerard Manley Hopkins, who had a profound sense of God's presence in the world around him, but also a deep awareness of the ambiguity of suffering and the challenge to religious belief and hope in the transformation of all things. He believed that 'I am all at once what Christ is, since he was what I am, and This Jack, joke, poor potsherd, patch, matchwood, immortal diamond, Is immortal diamond.'[10] Wonder on the spiritual journey can only hint at the reign of God; we have, with Aquinas, to wait for the beatific vision. Yet Hopkins' poetic imagination was also aware of the need for human responsibility for creation; creation as charged with God's glory is a vocation to love the earth as that which God has made. Our spirituality cannot be divorced from practice. Nor can the applications of science through technology remain responsible without practical wisdom.

God's Grandeur

The world is charged with the grandeur of God.
It will flame out, like shining from shook foil;
It gathers to a greatness, like the ooze of oil
Crushed. Why do men then now not reck his rod?
Generations have trod, have trod, have trod;
And all is seared with trade; bleared, smeared with toil;
And wears man's smudge and shares man's smell: the soil
Is bare now, nor can foot feel, being shod.

And for all this, nature is never spent;
There lives the dearest freshness deep down things;
And though the last lights off the black West went
Oh morning, at the brown brink eastward, springs –
Because the Holy Ghost over the bent
World broods with warm breast and ah! bright wings.[11]

BIBLIOGRAPHY

Aquinas, *Summa Theologiae, Volume 23, Virtue*, Ia2ae, translated by W. D. Hughes (London: Blackfriars, 1969).

Aquinas, *Summa Theologiae, Ia2ae, Volume 28, Law and Political Theory*, translated by Thomas Gilby (London: Blackfriars, 1966).

Aquinas, *Summa Theologiae, Volume 33, Hope*, IIa2ae, translated by W. J. Hill (London: Blackfriars, 1966).

Aquinas, *Summa Theologiae, Volume 34, Charity*, IIa2ae, translated by R. J. Batten (London; Blackfriars, 1975).

Armstrong, Patrick, *The English Parson–Naturalist: A Companionship Between Science and Religion* (Leominster: Gracewing, 2000).

Augustine, *Trinity*, VII.1.2; XV.7.12.

Berrill, N. J., *Journey into Wonder* (London: Victor Gollancz, 1953).

Bersanelli, M. and Gargantini, M., *Solo lo Stupore Conosce: L'Avventura Della Ricerca Scientifica* (Milano: Biblioteca Universale Rizzoli, 2003).

Bonaventure, *The Journey of the Mind to God*, translated by P. Boehner, edited by S. F. Brown (Indianapolis: Hackett Publishing, 1993).

Bonting, S. L., *Chaos Theology: A Revised Creation Theology* (Ottawa: Novalis, 2002).

Brockelman, Paul, *Cosmology and Creation: The Spiritual Significance of Contemporary Cosmology* (New York: Oxford University Press, 1999).

Brooke, J. H. and Cantor, G., *Reconstructing Nature: The Engagement of Science and Religion* (Edinburgh: T & T Clark, 1998).

Brown, David, *God and Enchantment of Place: Reclaiming Human Experience* (Oxford: Oxford University Press, 2004).

Brown, Warren S. (ed.), *Understanding Wisdom: Sources, Science and Society* (Philadelphia: Templeton Foundation Press, 2000).

Bulgakov, Sergei, *Sophia: The Wisdom of God* (Hudson: Lindisfarne Press, 1993).

Bulgakov, Sergei, *The Holy Grail and the Eucharist*, translated by Boris Jakim (Hudson: Lindisfarne Books, 1997).

Campbell, Mary Bruce, *Wonder and Science: Imagining Worlds in Early Modern Europe* (Ithaca and London: Cornell University Press, 1999).

Ceccarelli, Leah, *Shaping Science with Rhetoric: The Cases of Dobshansky, Schrödinger and Wilson* (Chicago and London: University of Chicago Press, 2001).

Chesterton, G. K., *The Defendant* (London: Dent, 1922).

Clayton, Philip and Peacocke, Arthur (eds.), *In Whom We Live, and Move and Have Our Being: Panentheistic Reflections on God's Presence in a Scientific World* (Grand Rapids: W. B. Eerdmans, 2004).

Clayton, Philip and Schloss, Jeffrey (eds.), *Evolution and Ethics: Human Morality in Biological and Religious Perspective* (Grand Rapids: W. B. Eerdmans, 2004).

Conradie, E., *An Ecological Christian Anthropology: At Home on Earth?* (Aldershot: Ashgate, 2005).

Conway Morris, Simon, *Life's Solution: Inevitable Humans in a Lonely Universe* (Cambridge: Cambridge University Press, 2003).

Cornwell, John (ed.), *Consciousness and Human Identity* (Oxford: Oxford University Press, 1998).

Daston, Lorraine and Park, Katherine, *Wonders and the Orders of Nature* (New York: Zone Books, 1998).

Davies, Paul, *The Mind of God: Science and the Search for Ultimate Meaning* (London: Simon and Schuster, 1992).

Davies, Paul, *The Cosmic Blueprint: New Discoveries in Nature's Creative Ability to Order the Universe*, 2nd Edition (Philadelphia: Templeton Foundation Press, 2004).

Dawkins, Richard, *Unweaving the Rainbow: Science, Delusion and the Appetite for Wonder* (London: Faber and Faber, 1998).

de Waal, Esther, *Lost in Wonder: Rediscovering the Spiritual Art of Attentiveness* (Norwich: Canterbury Press, 2003).

Deane-Drummond, Celia, *Creation through Wisdom: Theology and the New Biology* (Edinburgh: T & T Clark, 2000).

Deane-Drummond, Celia, *The Ethics of Nature* (Oxford: Blackwell, 2004).

Deane-Drummond, Celia, 'Where Streams Meet? Ecology, Wisdom and Beauty in Bulgakov, von Balthasar and Aquinas', Conference Proceedings of the European Society for the Study of Science and Theology (ESSSAT), 2004 Conference, *Issues in Science and Theology 4* (London: T & T Clark/Continuum, 2006) in press).

Dillard, Annie, *Pilgrim at Tinker Creek* (New York: Harpers' Magazine Press, Harper and Row, 1974).

Dowell, G., *Enjoying the World: The Rediscovery of Thomas Traherne* (London: Mowbray, 1990).

Drees, Willem B. (ed.), *Is Nature Ever Evil? Religion, Science and Value* (London: Routledge, 2003).

Dwyer, T., *The Motif of Wonder in the Gospel of Mark* (*Journal for the Study of the New Testament*, Supplement Series 128, Sheffield: Sheffield Academic Press, 1996).

Eco, U., *The Aesthetics of Thomas Aquinas*, translated by Hugh Bredin (Cambridge: Harvard University Press, 1988).

Edwards D. and Worthing, M., *Biodiversity and Ecology as Interdisciplinary Challenge* (Adelaide: ATF Press, 2004).

Edwards, D., *Breath of Life: A Theology of the Creator Spirit* (Maryknoll: Orbis, 2004).

Edwards, D., 'Every Sparrow That Falls to the Ground. The Cost of Evolution and the Christ-Event', *Ecotheology*, 11.1 (2006), in press.

Ewen, A. H. and Prime, T., (eds), *Ray's Flora of Cambridgeshire* (Hitchin: Wheldon and Wesley, 1975).

Farrer, A., *The Glass of Vision* (Westminster: Dacre Press, 1948).

Ford, David and Stanton, Graham (eds), *Reading Texts: Seeking Wisdom* (London: SCM Press, 2003).

Gardner, W. H., *Poems and Prose of Gerard Manley Hopkins* (London: Penguin Classics, 1985).

Gee, H., 'Flores, God and Cryptozoology', www.nature.com/news/2004/041025/full/041025-2.html.

Greenfield, Susan, *Journey to the Centres of the Mind* (New York: W. H. Freeman and Co, 1995).

Gregersen, N., 'The Cross of Christ in an Evolutionary World, *Dialog: A Journal of Theology*, 40 (2001), pp.192–207.

Gregersen, N. and Gorman, U., (eds), *Design and Disorder: Perspectives from Science and Theology* (London: T & T Clark, 2002).

Hart, David Bentley, *The Beauty of the Infinite* (Grand Rapids: W. B. Eerdmans, 2003).

Haught, John, *The Promise of Nature: Ecology and Cosmic Purpose* (New York: Paulist Press, 1993).

Hibbs, Thomas S., *Virtue's Splendor: Wisdom, Prudence and the Human Good* (New York: Fordham University Press, 2001).

Inge, Denise, *Thomas Traherne: Poetry and Prose* (London: SPCK, 2002).

Johnson, E. A., *She Who Is: The Mystery of God in Feminist Theological Discourse* (New York: Crossroad, 1992).

Keller, Evelyn Fox, *A Feeling for the Organism: The Life and Work of Barbara McClintock* (New York: Freeman, 1983).

Keselopoulus, Anestis G., *Man and the Environment: A Study of St Symeon the New Theologian*, translated by Elizabeth Theokritoff (Crestwood: St Vladimir's Seminary Press, 2001).

Lash, Nicholas, *Holiness, Speech and Silence: Reflections on the Question of God* (Aldershot: Ashgate, 2004).

Lash, Nicholas, *The Beginning and End of Religion* (Cambridge:

Cambridge University Press, 1996).

Lash, Nicholas, *Seeing in the Dark* (London: Darton, Longman and Todd, 2005).

Locker, Thomas and Bruchac, Joseph, *Rachel Carson: Preserving a Sense of Wonder* (Golden: Fulchrum Publishing, 2004).

Maslow, A. H., *Religion, Wonder and Peak Experiences* (New York: Viking, 1973).

Maxwell, Nicholas, *From Knowledge to Wisdom: A Revolution in the Aims and Methods of Science* (Oxford: Blackwell, 1984).

McGrath, A., *Dawkins' God: Genes, Memes and the Meaning of Life* (Oxford: Blackwell, 2005).

Midgley, Mary, *Wisdom, Information and Wonder: What is Knowledge For?* (London: Routledge, 1989).

Midgley, Mary, *Science and Poetry* (London: Routledge, 2001).

Miller, Jerome A., *In the Throe of Wonder: Intimations of the Sacred in a Post-Modern World* (Albany: State University of New York Press, 1992).

Moltmann, J., *The Crucified God*, translated by R. A. Wilson and J. Bowden (London: SCM Press, 1974).

Moltmann, J., *The Way of Jesus Christ*, translated by M. Kohl (London: SCM Press, 1990).

Moltmann, J., *The Coming of God: Christian Eschatology* (London: SCM Press, 1996).

Moltmann, J., *Science and Wisdom* (London: SCM Press, 2003).

Murphy, Nancey and Ellis, George, *On the Moral Nature of the Universe: Theology, Cosmology, and Ethics* (Minneapolis: Fortress Press, 1996), pp.52–3.

Murphy, R. E., *The Tree of Life: An Exploration of Biblical Wisdom Literature*, 2nd Edition (Grand Rapids: W. B. Eerdmans, 1996).

Nichols, Aidan, 'Wisdom from Above? The Sophiology of Father Sergius Bulgakov', *New Blackfriars*, Volume 85, November 2004, pp.598–613.

Northcott, M., 'Do Dolphins Carry the Cross? Biological Moral Realism and Theological Ethics', *New Blackfriars*, December 2003, pp.540–53.

Otto, Rudolf, *The Idea of the Holy: An Inquiry into the Non-Rational Factor in the Idea of the Divine and its Relation to the Rational*, translated by J. W. Harvey (Oxford: Oxford University Press, 1923).

Peacocke, Arthur, *Evolution: The Disguised Friend of Faith? Selected Essays* (Philadelphia: Templeton Foundation Press, 2004).

Pascal, B., *Pensées*, edited by Francis Kaplan (Paris: Editions du Cerf, 1992), 3, 206.

Peters, Ted; Russell, Robert J. and Welker, Michael (eds), *Resurrection:*

Theological and Scientific Assessments (Grand Rapids: W. B. Eerdmans, 2002).

Polkinghorne, J. (ed.), *The Work of Love: Creation as Kenosis* (Grand Rapids: W. B. Eerdmans, 2001), pp.1–20.

Polkinghorne, J., *The God of Hope and the End of the World* (London: SPCK, 2002).

Popa, R., *Between Necessity and Probability: Searching for the Definition and Origin of Life* (Berlin/Heidelberg: Springer-Verlag, 2004).

Randall, Lisa, *Warped Passages* (New York: Allen Lane, 2005).

Raven, Charles, *John Ray: Naturalist* (Cambridge: Cambridge University Press, 1942).

Rees, Martin, *Our Cosmic Habitat* (Princeton: Princeton University Press, 2001).

Rolston, H. (ed.), *Biology, Ethics and the Origin of Life* (Boston: Jones and Bartlett Publishers, 1995).

Rossano, Matthew J., *Evolutionary Psychology: The Science of Human Behaviour and Evolution* (London: John Wiley, 2003).

Seidenspinner-Minez, Dayle (trans.), *The Writings of Teresa de Cartegena*, (Cambridge: D. S. Brewer, 1998).

Sigrist, S., *Theology of Wonder* (Crestwood: St Vladimir's Seminary Press, 1999).

Sorrell, Roger D., *St Francis of Assisi and Nature: Tradition and Innovation in Western Christian Attitudes Toward the Environment* (Oxford: Oxford University Press, 1988).

Southgate, Christopher, 'God and Evolutionary Evil: Theodicy in the Light of Darwinism', *Zygon*, 37 (2002), 803–22.

Stannard, R., (ed.), *Science and Wonders: Conversations About Science and Belief* (London: Faber and Faber, 1996).

Sternberg, Robert J. (ed.), *Wisdom: Its Nature, Origin and Development* (Cambridge: Cambridge University Press, 1990).

Swimme, Brian and Berry, Thomas, *The Universe Story: From the Primordial Flaring Forth to the Ecozoic Era: A Celebration of The Unfolding of the Cosmos* (New York: Harper Collins, 1992).

Szerszynski, Bronisław, *Nature, Technology and the Sacred* (Oxford: Blackwell, 2005).

Teilhard de Chardin, Pierre, *The Human Phenomenon*, translated by Sarah Appleton-Weber (Brighton: Sussex University Press, 1999), pp.22–38.

Teilhard de Chardin, Pierre, *The Divine Milieu*, translated by Siôn Cowell (Brighton: Sussex University Press, 2004).

Thwaite, Ann, *Glimpses of the Wonderful: The Life of Philip Henry Gosse* (London: Faber and Faber, 2002).

Ulmschneider, Peter, *Intelligent Life in the Universe: From Common*

Origins to the Future of Humanity (Berlin/Heidelberg/New York: Springer-Verlag, 2003).

Vardy, Peter, *Being Human: Fulfilling Genetic and Spiritual Potential* (London: Darton, Longman and Todd, 2002).

von Balthasar, Hans urs, *The Glory of the Lord: A Theological Aesthetics*, *Vol. 1: Seeing the Form*, Erasmo Leiva-Merikakis (trans.) and Joseph Fessio (ed.) (London: T & T Clark, 1982).

von Balthasar, Hans urs, *The Glory of the Lord: A Theological Aesthetics*, *Volume 2: Studies in Theological Style: Clerical Styles*, Andrew Louth, Francis McDonough and Brian McNeil, (trans.), John Riches (ed.) (London: T & T Clark, 1984).

Weil, Simone, *Gravity and Grace*, with Introduction by Gustave Thibon (London: Routledge and Kegan Paul, 1952).

Wilson, E. O., *On Human Nature* (Cambridge, MA: Harvard University Press, 1978).

Wilson, E. O., *Biophilia: The Human Bond with Other Species* (Cambridge, MA: Harvard University Press, 1984).

Wilson, E. O., *In Search of Nature* (Washington Island Press, Shearwater Books, 1996).

Wilson, E. O., *Consilience* (London: Abacus, 1999).

Woodhead, Linda, 'Earthly Power Behind the Divine Glory', *The Times Higher Educational Supplement*, 18 March, 2005, pp.20–21.

Wright, M. R., *Cosmology in Antiquity* (London: Routledge, 1995).

Zizioulas, J., *Being as Communion* (London: Darton, Longman and Todd, 2004).

NOTES

Introduction

1. For a comprehensive study of the early history of the meaning of wonder see Lorraine Daston and Katherine Park, *Wonders and the Orders of Nature* (New York: Zone Books, 1998). See especially pp.23–50 and pp.291–367.
2. Ibid., p.306
3. Ibid., p.312.
4. Ibid., p.326.
5. Curiosity also became associated with greed and avarice, but these were channelled in such a way to good effect; in other words, not greed in the more obvious sense of the word, but one that could be linked with a new respectability.
6. Adam Smith was exceptional in arguing for recovering the idea of wonder as the start of philosophy, focusing particularly on the possible role of wonder in the history of astronomy.
7. Daston and Park, *Wonders and the Orders of Nature*, p.304.
8. Ibid., p.305.
9. Mary Bruce Campbell, *Wonder and Science: Imagining Worlds in Early Modern Europe* (Ithaca and London: Cornell University Press, 1999), p.4.
10. Daston and Park, *Wonders and the Orders of Nature*, p.361.
11. Cited as acknowledgement at beginning of Jerome A. Miller, *In the Throe of Wonder: Intimations of the Sacred in a Post-Modern World* (Albany: State University of New York Press, 1992).
12. Ibid., p.xii.
13. Ibid., p.3.
14. Ibid., p.6.
15. Ibid., p.7.
16. This book also illustrates, perhaps, a turn in the fortune of wonder – that it is now becoming more acceptable for scientists to admit to wonder in the course of their work. M. Bersanelli and M. Gargantini,

[172]

Solo lo Stupore Conosce: L'Avventura Della Ricerca Scientifica (Milano: Biblioteca Universale Rizzoli, 2003).

17. For a survey of wisdom in religious writing, science and learning see Warren S. Brown (ed.), *Understanding Wisdom: Sources, Science and Society* (Philadelphia: Templeton Foundation Press, 2000).

18. Nancey Murphy, 'Introduction: A Hierarchical Framework for Understanding Wisdom', in Brown (ed.), *Understanding Wisdom*, pp.1–11.

19. M. Midgley, *Wisdom, Information and Wonder: What is Knowledge For?* (London: Routledge, 1989).

20. N. Lash, *The Beginning and End of Religion* (Cambridge: Cambridge University Press, 1996), pp.116–7.

21. N. Maxwell, *From Knowledge to Wisdom: A Revolution in the Aims and Methods of Science* (Oxford: Blackwell, 1984).

22. R. E. Murphy, *The Tree of Life: An Exploration of Biblical Wisdom Literature*, 2nd Edition (Grand Rapids: W. B. Eerdmans, 1996).

23. J. P. Schloss, 'Wisdom Traditions as Mechanisms for Organismal Integration: Evolutionary Perspectives on Homeostatic "Laws of Life"', in Brown (ed.), *Understanding Wisdom*, pp.153–91.

24. Ibid. p.156.

25. E. O. Wilson, *On Human Nature* (Cambridge, MA: Harvard University Press, 1978).

26. E. J. Ayala, 'The Difference of Being Human: Ethical Behaviour as an Evolutionary By-product', in H. Rolston (ed.), *Biology, Ethics and the Origin of Life* (Boston: Jones and Bartlett Publishers, 1995), pp.113–36.

27. The technical term for this layering is tertiary heuristic. If learning represents the secondary heuristic, then culture represents the tertiary heuristic.

28. Schloss, 'Wisdom Traditions', p.166.

29. Warren S. Brown, 'Wisdom and Human Neurocognitive Systems: Perceiving and Practising the Laws of Life', in Brown (ed.), *Understanding Wisdom*, p.194.

30. Miller, *In the Throe of Wonder*, p.37.

31. Simone Weil, *Gravity and Grace*, with Introduction by Gustave Thibon (London: Routledge and Kegan Paul, 1952), p.105.

32. Ibid., p.106.

33. Ibid., p.106.

34. Linda Woodhead, 'Earthly Power Behind the Divine Glory', *The Times Higher Educational Supplement*, 18 March 2005, pp.20–21.

35. Midgley, *Wisdom, Information and Wonder*, p.41.

Chapter 1: Wonderful World

1. See useful discussion in, for example, M. R. Wright, *Cosmology in Antiquity* (London: Routledge, 1995).
2. Martin Rees, *Our Cosmic Habitat* (Princeton: Princeton University Press, 2001), pp.65–86.
3. Paul Davies, *The Mind of God: Science and the Search for Ultimate Meaning* (London: Simon and Schuster, 1992), pp.196–7.
4. Rees, *Our Cosmic Habitat*, p.81.
5. Ibid., p.89.
6. Einstein's general theory of relativity is a theory of gravitation which describes effects in terms of the curvature of space–time.
7. Davies, *The Mind of God*, p.195.
8. Ibid., p.205. See also P. Davies, *The Cosmic Blueprint: New Discoveries in Nature's Creative Ability to Order the Universe*, 2nd Edition (Philadelphia: Templeton Foundation Press, 2004).
9. P. Davies, cited in R. Stannard (ed.), *Science and Wonders: Conversations About Science and Belief* (London: Faber and Faber, 1996), p.20.
10. Some cosmologists have raised the possibility recently that the so-called 'laws' of nature in the universe may not have always been the same, in other words, there might have been a change in physical laws over time. The implications of this possibility, if found to be true, are staggering, and might imply an 'evolutionary' path towards the present laws, rather than fixation of the laws in the beginning. How such laws came to take precedence over other laws, perhaps less favourable for life, would still be a matter of conjecture.
11. Nancey Murphy and George Ellis, *On the Moral Nature of the Universe: Theology, Cosmology, and Ethics* (Minneapolis: Fortress Press, 1996), pp.52–3.
12. Peter Ulmschneider, *Intelligent Life in the Universe: From Common Origins to the Future of Humanity* (Berlin/Heidelberg/New York: Springer-Verlag, 2003).
13. See Rees, *Our Cosmic Habitat*, and also Stannard, *Science and Wonders*, pp.4–31.
14. P. Atkins, cited in Stannard, *Science and Wonders*, p.25.
15. P. Davies, cited in ibid., p.24.
16. B. Russell, cited in ibid., p.31.
17. T. Cech, 'The Origin of Life and the Value of Life', in H. Rolston, *Biology, Ethics and the Origin of Life*, pp.18–37.
18. R. Popa, *Between Necessity and Probability: Searching for the Definition and Origin of Life* (Berlin/Heidelberg: Springer-Verlag, 2004).
19. Paul Brockelman, *Cosmology and Creation: The Spiritual*

Significance of Contemporary Cosmology (New York: Oxford University Press, 1999), pp.55–64.

20. H. Gee, 'Flores, God and Cryptozoology', www.nature.com/news/2004/041025/full/041025-2.html.

21. These figures are approximate only; they may have lived earlier than this, or somewhat later as well.

22. Richard Leakey, cited in Brockelman, *Cosmology and Creation*, pp.4–5.

23. Ibid., p.49.

24. Ibid., p.71. For discussion on 'paying attention', see previous Introduction.

25. P. Teilhard de Chardin, *The Human Phenomenon*, translated by Sarah Appleton-Weber (Brighton: Sussex University Press, 1999), pp.22–38.

26. John Haught, *The Promise of Nature: Ecology and Cosmic Purpose* (New York: Paulist Press, 1993).

27. B. Swimme and T. Berry, *The Universe Story: From the Primordial Flaring Forth to the Ecozoic Era: A Celebration of the Unfolding of the Cosmos* (New York: Harper Collins, 1992), esp. pp.7–79.

28. Ibid., p.70. Although scientists have discovered that this capacity is related to the precise 'roughness' of the Big Bang, the question still haunts as to why this is the case.

29. Ibid., p.74.

30. J. Polkinghorne, *The God of Hope and the End of the World* (London: SPCK, 2002).

31. Sjoerd Bonting argues that *creatio ex nihilo*, the doctrine of creation out of nothing, is no longer sustainable in the light of modern cosmology and physics. S. L. Bonting, *Chaos Theology: A Revised Creation Theology* (Ottawa: Novalis, 2002).

32. Bonting argues contrary to this, that the chaos in Genesis echoes that of the Big Bang, and that the unfolding story of the text has its scientific parallels, p.26–8.

33. I will come back to this again in the discussion of *God as Wisdom* in Chapter 5.

Chapter 2: Wonderful Life

1. See M. Bersanelli and M. Gargantini, *Solo Lo Stupore Conosce: L'Avventura Della Ricerca Scientifica*.

2. Roger D. Sorrell, *St Francis of Assisi and Nature: Tradition and Innovation in Western Christian Attitudes Toward the Environment* (Oxford: Oxford University Press, 1988), pp.94–124.

3. Patrick Armstrong, *The English Parson-Naturalist: A Companionship Between Science and Religion* (Leominster: Gracewing, 2000), p.2.

4. Preface for the Reader in *Catalogus Plantarum circa Cantabrigiam nascentium*, A. H. Ewen and T. Prime (eds), *Ray's Flora of Cambridgeshire* (Hitchin: Wheldon and Wesley, 1975), p.22.
5. Armstrong, *The English Parson-Naturalist*, p.48.
6. Charles Raven, *John Ray: Naturalist* (Cambridge: Cambridge University Press, 1942), p.193.
7. N. J. Berrill, *Journey into Wonder* (London: Victor Gollancz, 1953), p.239.
8. A. R. Wallace, for example, wrote *The Wonderful Century* in 1889. Cited in Ann Thwaite, *Glimpses of the Wonderful: The Life of Philip Henry Gosse* (London: Faber and Faber, 2002), p.362, note 209.
9. Thwaite, *Glimpses of the Wonderful*, p.215.
10. E. O. Wilson, *Biophilia: The Human Bond with Other Species* (Cambridge, MA: Harvard University Press, 1984), p.1.
11. See, for example, M. Midgley, *Science and Poetry* (London: Routledge, 2001).
12. E. O. Wilson, *Consilience* (London: Abacus, 1999).
13. Leah Ceccarelli, *Shaping Science with Rhetoric: The Cases of Dobshansky, Schrödinger and Wilson* (Chicago and London: University of Chicago Press, 2001), p.128.
14. Ibid., p.138.
15. E. O. Wilson, *In Search of Nature* (Washington: Island Press, Shearwater Books, 1996), p.174.
16. Rachel Carson, *Silent Spring* (Boston: Houghton Mifflin, 1961).
17. A beautifully illustrated book is Thomas Locker and Joseph Bruchac's *Rachel Carson: Preserving a Sense of Wonder* (Golden: Fulchrum Publishing, 2004).
18. Cited in ibid., p.32.
19. Annie Dillard, *Pilgrim at Tinker Creek* (New York: Harpers' Magazine Press, Harper and Row, 1974), p.3.
20. Richard Dawkins, *Unweaving the Rainbow: Science, Delusion and the Appetite for Wonder* (London: Faber and Faber, 1998), p.17.
21. For clear exposition of Dawkins' misapprehensions in this respect, see A. McGrath, *Dawkins' God: Genes, Memes and the Meaning of Life* (Oxford: Blackwell, 2005), pp.146–50.
22. Nicholas Lash is particularly critical of what he calls the 'spectatorial' view of the universe promoted by science. N. Lash, *The Beginning and End of Religion*, p.92.
23. Evelyn Fox Keller, *A Feeling for the Organism: The Life and Work of Barbara McClintock* (New York: Freeman, 1983).
24. T. King, Foreword to Pierre Teilhard de Chardin, *The Divine Milieu*, translated by Siôn Cowell (Brighton: Sussex University Press, 2004), p.xxiv.

25. Ibid., p.75.
26. H. Gee, 'Flores, God and Cryptozoology'.
27. Ibid.

Chapter 3: Natural Wisdom

1. Bonaventure, *The Journey of the Mind to God*, translated by P. Boehner, edited by S. F. Brown (Indianapolis: Hackett Publishing, 1993), Chapter 1.10–12, p.8.
2. Ibid., Chapter 1.8, p.7.
3. Ibid., Chapter 2.1, p.11.
4. Ibid., Prologue, 4, p.2. See also pp.70–1 for commentary. The mirror in this context refers to the mirror of the external world, but such a mirror is 'of little or no avail unless the mirror of our soul has been cleansed and polished'.
5. Recent editions of both these works are now available. See P. Teilhard de Chardin, *The Human Phenomenon* and P. Teilhard de Chardin, *The Divine Milieu*.
6. A. Peacocke, *Evolution: The Disguised Friend of Faith? Selected Essays* (Philadelphia: Templeton Foundation Press, 2004).
7. See J. H. Brooke and G. Cantor, *Reconstructing Nature: The Engagement of Science and Religion* (Edinburgh: T & T Clark, 1998), p.95.
8. Thomas Traherne, *The Centuries of Meditations*, The Third Century, 2 line 17, in Denise Inge, *Thomas Traherne: Poetry and Prose* (London: SPCK, 2002), p.16.
9. Ibid., The Third Century, 16 line 5–8, p.23.
10. Ibid., pp.57–63.
11. Traherne, *Christian Ethicks*, cited in G. Dowell, *Enjoying the World: The Rediscovery of Thomas Traherne* (London: Mowbray, 1990), p.55.
12. I am grateful to Norman Habel for this insight. See, for example, N. Habel, 'Design, Diversity and Dominion: Biodiversity and Job 39', in D. Edwards and M. Worthing, *Biodiversity and Ecology as Interdisciplinary Challenge* (Adelaide: ATF Press, 2004), pp.55–71.
13. Also commented upon by Paul Joyce in 'Proverbs 8 in Interpretation (1): Historical Criticism and Beyond', in David Ford and Graham Stanton (eds), *Reading Texts, Seeking Wisdom* (London: SCM Press, 2003), pp.89–101.
14. Habel, 'Design, Diversity and Dominion', p.59.
15. S. Conway Morris, *Life's Solution: Inevitable Humans in a Lonely Universe* (Cambridge: Cambridge University Press, 2003), p.9.
16. Ibid., p.20.
17. Simon Conway Morris's book *Life's Solution* is full of excellent

examples of this phenomenon. The examples discussed here are taken from this source.

18. G. K. Chesterton, *The Defendant* (London: Dent, 1922), p.134
19. A discussion of how this version of natural law theory differs from other possible versions is outside the scope of this book.

Chapter 4: Human Wisdom

1. Susan Greenfield, *Journey to the Centres of the Mind* (New York: W. H. Freeman and Co., 1995); John Cornwell (ed.), *Consciousness and Human Identity* (Oxford: Oxford University Press, 1998).
2. See also previous chapter. S. Conway Morris, *Life's Solution*.
3. Ibid., p.253.
4. Matthew J. Rossano, *Evolutionary Psychology: The Science of Human Behaviour and Evolution* (London: John Wiley, 2003).
5. See Introduction for further discussion of this aspect.
6. Mihaly Csikszentmihalyi and Kevin Rathunde, 'The Psychology of Wisdom: An Evolutionary Interpretation', in Robert J. Sternberg (ed.), *Wisdom: Its Nature, Origin and Development* (Cambridge; Cambridge University Press, 1990). See also Warren Brown, *Understanding Wisdom: Sources, Science and Society* (Philadelphia: Templeton Foundation Press, 2000).
7. Detailed discussion of these debates is outside the scope of this book. For more detail and an overview of different positions, see Philip Clayton and Jeffrey Schloss (eds), *Evolution and Ethics: Human Morality in Biological and Religious Perspective* (Grand Rapids: W.B. Eerdmans, 2004).
8. Peter Vardy, *Being Human: Fulfilling Genetic and Spiritual Potential* (London: Darton, Longman and Todd, 2002), p.145.
9. Nicholas Lash, 'Recovering Contingency', in John Cornwell (ed.), *Consciousness and Human Identity*, pp.197–211.
10. Ibid., p.204.
11. Ibid., p.205.
12. R. E. Murphy, *The Tree of Life: An Exploration of Biblical Wisdom Literature*, 2nd Edition.
13. I will develop in more detail the theological basis for the Wisdom of the cross in a later chapter.
14. Jeffrey Schloss is aware of this difficulty as it applies to practices such as celibacy. See, for example, his 'Introduction' in Clayton and Schloss, *Evolution and Ethics*, pp.1–26.
15. Aquinas, *Summa Theologiae, Volume 23, Virtue*, translated by W. D. Hughes (London: Blackfriars, 1969), Ia2ae, Qu. 57.
16. I will be coming back to the concepts of how God works in the world through wisdom, and the human journey into wonder in chapter 5

and chapter 7 respectively.

17. Aquinas, *Summa Theologiae, Volume 33, Hope*, translated by W. J. Hill (London: Blackfriars, 1966), IIa2ae, Qu. 19.7.

18. Aquinas, *Summa Theologiae, Volume 34, Charity*, translated by R. J. Batten (London: Blackfriars, 1975), IIa2ae, Qu. 23.2.

Chapter 5: God as Wisdom

1. I deal with some of the material covered in this chapter in more depth in C. Deane-Drummond, *Creation through Wisdom: Theology and the New Biology* (Edinburgh: T & T Clark, 2000).

2. The Hebrew scholar Norman Habel favours this translation, as I discussed in more detail in chapter 3.

3. J. Moltmann, *Science and Wisdom* (London: SCM Press, 2003), p.150.

4. This is a view adopted by those who subscribe to process theology, but also others. See earlier discussion in chapter 1 and Sjoerd Bonting, *Chaos Theology: A Revised Creation Theology* (Ottawa: Novalis, 2002).

5. Nicholas Lash, *Holiness, Speech and Silence: Reflections on the Question of God* (Aldershot: Ashgate, 2004), pp.77–85.

6. Aquinas, *Summa Theologiae, Volume 28, Law and Political Theory*, translated by Thomas Gilby (London: Blackfriars, 1966), Ia2ae, Qu. 93.1.

7. Moltmann, *Science and Wisdom*, p.151.

8. Aquinas, *Summa Theologiae, Volume 28, Law and Political Theory*, Ia2ae, Qu. 93.1.

9. For more detail see Niels Henrik Gregersen, 'Beyond the Balance: Theology in a Self-Organising World', in N. Gregersen and U. Gorman (eds), *Design and Disorder: Perspectives from Science and Theology* (London: T & T Clark, 2002), pp.53–91.

10. See chapter 3 for more discussion of convergence.

11. Denis Edwards equates wisdom with the figure of Christ in his *Jesus: the Wisdom of God* (Maryknoll: Orbis, 1995).

12. For some detailed exegetical discussions see Morna D. Hooker, 'Where is Wisdom to be Found? Colossians 1:15–20 (1)', in D. Ford and G. Stanton (eds), *Reading Texts: Seeking Wisdom* (London: SCM Press, 2003), pp.116–28 and R. Bauckham, 'Where is Wisdom to be Found? Colossians 1:15–20 (2)' in Ford and Stanton, *Reading Texts: Seeking Wisdom*, pp.129–38.

13. For a more detailed argument see C. Deane-Drummond, 'The Logos as Wisdom: A Starting Point for a Sophianic Theology of Creation', in Philip Clayton and Arthur Peacocke (eds), *In Whom We Live, and Move and Have Our Being: Panentheistic Reflections on God's Presence in a Scientific World* (Grand Rapids: W. B. Eerdmans, 2004), pp.233–45.

14. Augustine, *Trinity*, VII.1.2; XV.7.12.
15. J. Moltmann, *The Way of Jesus Christ*, translated by M. Kohl (London: SCM Press, 1990), p.289.
16. D. Edwards, *Breath of Life: A Theology of the Creator Spirit* (Maryknoll: Orbis, 2004).
17. Ibid., p.48.
18. Moltmann, *Science and Wisdom*, footnote 12, p.209.
19. For fuller comparison between these authors see C. Deane-Drummond, 'Where Streams Meet? Ecology, Wisdom and Beauty in Bulgakov, von Balthasar and Aquinas', Conference Proceedings of the European Society for the Study of Science and Theology (ESSSAT) 2004, *Issues in Science and Theology 4*, (London: T & T Clark, 2006, *in press*).
20. Sergei Bulgakov, *Sophia: The Wisdom of God* (Hudson: Lindisfarne Press, 1993).
21. In technical jargon this tradition is known as the *apophatic* tradition. The tradition that allows us to speak about God is known as the *cataphatic* tradition.
22. Lash, *Holiness, Speech and Silence*.
23. For more discussion of this theme see Deane-Drummond, *Creation through Wisdom*, pp.131–7.
24. E. A. Johnson, *She Who Is: The Mystery of God in Feminist Theological Discourse* (New York: Crossroad, 1992).
25. For further discussion of this idea see J. Zizioulas, *Being as Communion* (London: Darton, Longman and Todd, 2004).

Chapter 6: Crucified Wisdom

1. In this I agree with Ernst Conradie and others that mortality as such cannot be considered an evil. E. Conradie, *An Ecological Christian Anthropology: At Home on Earth?* (Aldershot: Ashgate, 2005), pp.44–51.
2. Consider the example of Jesus' healing of the man blind from birth, compared with the paralysed man by the pool. In the first case, Jesus rejects the explanation that suffering is an outcome of sin, but concedes this in the second case. Compare John 9:1–41 and John 5:1–16.
3. For more discussion see Willem B. Drees (ed.), *Is Nature Ever Evil? Religion, Science and Value* (London: Routledge, 2003).
4. S. Bonting, *Chaos Theology: A Revised Creation Theology* (Ottawa: Novalis, 2003).
5. Ibid., p.25.
6. B. Pascal, *Pensées*, Francis Kaplan (ed.) (Paris: Editions du Cerf, 1992), 3.206.

7. N. Gregersen, 'The Cross of Christ in an Evolutionary World', *Dialog: A Journal of Theology*, 40 (2001), 192–207.
8. See J. Moltmann, *The Crucified God*, translated by R. A. Wilson and J. Bowden (London: SCM Press, 1974). In as much as Christ suffers and dies, so God suffers, and the Holy Spirit also suffers by participation in the Trinity. I prefer to see the suffering of the Father as in some way analogous to the parent suffering for the sake of the child. But this is radically different from human suffering, in that God does not change because God loves eternally. Nicholas Lash believes that saying God suffers implies change, but this assumes suffering in God is equivalent to that found in humans, which it is not. See Nicholas Lash, *Holiness, Speech and Silence*, pp.67–9.
9. C. Deane-Drummond, *Creation through Wisdom*, pp.48–59.
10. H. Rolston, 'Naturalising and Systematising Evil', in W. B. Drees (ed.), *Is Nature Ever Evil?*, pp.83–5.
11. Ibid., p.84.
12. D. Edwards, *Breath of Life: A Theology of the Creator Spirit*, pp.109–110.
13. See previous chapter for a fuller account.
14. Edwards, *Breath of Life*, p.112.
15. Ibid., p.114.
16. D. Edwards, 'Every Sparrow That Falls to the Ground. The Cost of Evolution and the Christ-Event', *Ecotheology*, 11.1 (2006), in press.
17. J. Moltmann, *The Way of Jesus Christ*, p.303.
18. J. Moltmann, *The Coming of God: Christian Eschatology* (London: SCM Press, 1996), p.265. Edwards suggests that Moltmann's thinking has shifted in his later work, so that he speaks subsequently more about the transformation of the present creation in Christ. This is not so obvious to me; rather, Moltmann is insistent in this work, as he has been before, that there is no pristine beginning, but rather that there is a renewal of all things, even from the beginning.
19. Ibid., pp.338–9.
20. Ian Barbour, 'God's Power: A Process View', in J. Polkinghorne (ed.), *The Work of Love: Creation as Kenosis* (Grand Rapids: W. B. Eerdmans, 2001), pp.1–20.
21. Ernst Conradie, 'Resurrection, Finitude and Ecology', in Ted Peters, Robert J. Russell and Michael Welker (eds), *Resurrection: Theological and Scientific Assessments* (Grand Rapids: W. B. Eerdmans, 2002), pp.277–96. See also, Conradie, *An Ecological Christian Anthropology*, pp.166–9.
22. Edwards, D., 'Every Sparrow that Falls to the Ground: the Cost of Evolution and the Christ-Event' *Ecotheology*, 12.2 [2006].
23. Ibid.

24. J. Polkinghorne, *The God of Hope and the End of the World* (London: SPCK, 2002).
25. Ibid., pp.115–6.
26. Ibid., pp.122–3.
27. Further discussion of this issue is in C. Deane-Drummond, *The Ethics of Nature* (Oxford: Blackwell, 2004), pp.54–85.
28. M. Northcott, 'Do Dolphins Carry the Cross? Biological Moral Realism and Theological Ethics', *New Blackfriars*, December 2003, 540–53.
29. Such a view is clear in Andrew Linzey's account. For further discussion see Deane-Drummond, *The Ethics of Nature*, pp.62–5.
30. A suggestion made by Christopher Southgate, 'God and Evolutionary Evil: Theodicy in the Light of Darwinism', *Zygon*, 37 (2002), pp.803–22.
31. Nicholas Lash, *Holiness, Speech and Silence*, p.65.
32. Ibid., p.69.
33. Ibid., p.76.

Chapter 7: Journey into Wonder
1. David Brown discusses this type of experience in his book *God and Enchantment of Place: Reclaiming Human Experience* (Oxford: Oxford University Press, 2004), pp.84–152.
2. Thomas S. Hibbs, *Virtue's Splendor: Wisdom, Prudence and the Human Good* (New York: Fordham University Press, 2001), p.164.
3. In this respect at least, I agree with David Brown, *God and Enchantment of Place*, p.413.
4. I am drawing on Timothy Dwyer for this discussion on wonder, T. Dwyer, *The Motif of Wonder in the Gospel of Mark* (*Journal for the Study of the New Testament*, Supplement Series 128, Sheffield: Sheffield Academic Press, 1996).
5. A. H. Maslow, *Religion, Wonder and Peak Experiences* (New York: Viking, 1973).
6. Dwyer, *The Motif of Wonder*, pp.22–3.
7. Ibid., p.195.
8. Rudolf Otto, *The Idea of the Holy: An Inquiry into the Non-Rational Factor in the Idea of the Divine and its Relation to the Rational*, translated by J. W. Harvey (Oxford: Oxford University Press, 1923).
9. A danger vigorously resisted by Nicholas Lash in *Holiness, Speech and Silence*, pp.9–21.
10. Lash, 'Recovering Contingency', in John Cornwell (ed.), *Consciousness and Human Identity*, pp.208–9.
11. Lash, *Holiness, Speech and Silence*, p.44.
12. Ibid., p.15 and A. Farrer, *The Glass of Vision* (Westminster: Dacre Press, 1948), p.7.

13. Farrer, *Glass of Vision*, p.32.
14. Ibid., p.40.
15. Ibid., p.66.
16. Ibid., p.68.
17. Ibid., p.88.
18. Ibid., p.90.
19. S. Sigrist, *Theology of Wonder* (Crestwood: St Vladimir's Seminary Press, 1999).
20. Cited in ibid., p.37.
21. Ibid., p.132.
22. S. Bulgakov, *The Holy Grail and the Eucharist*, translated by Boris Jakim (Hudson: Lindisfarne Books, 1997), p.34.
23. Teresa de Cartegena, 'Wonder at the Works of God', in *The Writings of Teresa de Cartegena*, translated by Dayle Seidenspinner-Minez (Cambridge: D. S. Brewer, 1998).
24. Ibid., p.89.
25. Ibid., p.89.
26. Ibid., p.92.
27. Ibid., p.97.
28. Ibid., p.105.
29. Esther de Waal, *Lost in Wonder: Rediscovering the Spiritual Art of Attentiveness* (Norwich: Canterbury Press, 2003).
30. David Bentley Hart, *The Beauty of the Infinite* (Grand Rapids: W. B. Eerdmans, 2003).
31. Ibid., p.20.
32. Bonaventure, *Hineranum* 1.15, cited in ibid., p.309.
33. Paul Davies, *The Mind of God: Science and the Search for Ultimate Meaning* (London: Simon and Schuster, 1992), pp.175–6.
34. See Thomas S. Hibbs, *Virtue's Splendor: Wisdom, Prudence and the Human Good*.
35. Ibid., p.198.
36. Umberto Eco interprets Aquinas as denying the possibility of aesthetic vision in humans, based on human lack of knowledge. Hibbs, correctly in my view, rejects this idea, for it goes against Thomas' natural philosophy, that some knowledge at least is attainable, even if it is not complete. Ibid., pp.203–4 and U. Eco, *The Aesthetics of Thomas Aquinas*, translated by Hugh Bredin (Cambridge: Harvard University Press, 1988).
37. Anestis G. Keselopoulus, *Man and the Environment: A Study of St Symeon the New Theologian*, translated by Elizabeth Theokritoff (Crestwood: St Vladimir's Seminary Press, 2001), pp.19–21.
38. Ibid., p.20, note 21.
39. Sergei Bulgakov, *Sophia: The Wisdom of God: An Outline of*

Sophiology (Hudson): Lindisfarne Press, 1993), p.71.

40. Hans urs von Balthasar, *The Glory of the Lord: A Theological Aesthetics, Vol. 1: Seeing the Form*, Erasmo Leiva-Merikakis (trans.) and Joseph Fessio (ed.) (London: T & T Clark, 1982), p.679.
41. Hans urs von Balthasar, *The Glory of the Lord: A Theological Aesthetics, Vol. 2: Studies in Theological Style: Clerical Styles*, Andrew Louth, Francis McDonough and Brian McNeil (trans.) and John Riches (ed.) (London: T & T Clark, 1984), p.347.
42. Lash, 'Recovering Contingency', pp.207–8.

Chapter 8: Weaving Wonder and Wisdom

1. Daniel Hardy uses this term to describe the way Scripture needs to hold together diverse interpretations, including contact with the liturgy. Daniel Hardy, 'Reason, Wisdom and the Interpretation of Scripture', in Ford and Stanton (eds), *Reading Texts: Seeking Wisdom*, pp.69–88.
2. David Ford, 'Jesus Christ, the Wisdom of God (1)', in Ford and Stanton (eds), *Reading Texts: Seeking Wisdom*, p.4, full article, pp.4–21.
3. Lisa Randall has suggested that there are extra dimensions of space that have not so far been acknowledged by contemporary physics. L. Randall, *Warped Passages* (New York: Allen Lane, 2005).
4. As discussed in A. Nichols, 'Wisdom From Above? The Sophiology of Father Sergius Bulgakov', *New Blackfriars*, Vol 85, November 2004, 598–613.
5. Ibid., p.604.
6. R. Bauckham, 'Where is Wisdom to be Found? Colossians 1:15–20 (2)', in Ford and Stanton (eds), *Reading Texts: Seeking Wisdom*, p.138, full article, pp.129–38.
7. See C. Deane-Drummond, *Theology and Biotechnology: Implications for a New Science* (London: Cassell, 1997); C. Deane-Drummond, *The Ethics of Nature* (Oxford: Blackwell, 2004).
8. See especially Bronislaw Szerszynski, *Nature, Technology and the Sacred* (Oxford: Blackwell, 2005), p.x.
9. Ibid., p.171. A full discussion is outside the scope of this book.
10. From 'That Nature is a Heraclitean Fire and of the Comfort of the Resurrection', No.49, in W. H. Gardner, *Poems and Prose of Gerard Manley Hopkins* (London: Penguin Classics, 1985), p.65.
11. No.8 in ibid.

INDEX